The True Competitive Advantage

A Practical Guide to Achieving
Extraordinary Success
through Deep Relationships

DAN SILVERT

LIONCREST
PUBLISHING

THE TRUE COMPETITIVE ADVANTAGE

A Practical Guide to Achieving Extraordinary
Success through Deep Relationships

ISBN   978-1-61961-856-5 *Paperback*

978-1-61961-855-8 *Ebook*

THE TRUE COMPETITIVE ADVANTAGE

For Shaindelle, the joy of my life.

Contents

——

Introduction

This book is designed to help you advance your professional life by improving the relationships that surround you. Whether you're an employee a few years removed from college, a senior executive, or somewhere in between, we have found those who prioritize their relationship-building skills advance further and faster than those who focus solely on their technical expertise or specialized knowledge.

While understanding the art and science of people and relationships has always been important, the last ten years has featured an astounding acceleration of technology as an inhibitor of traditional relationship building from childhood through our working years. Essentially, our mobile devices and social media habits have radically altered the way one person gets to know another person. While virtual communication opens up a near infinite range of possible interactions, the price paid is often limited emotional connection and depth.

What hasn't changed, however, is this: forging deep bonds is essential to our happiness, our career success, and our physical health. While this book is not targeted to a particular generation, it is worth noting that actual relationship skills are more needed than ever in a world becoming increasingly virtual.

The True Competitive Advantage is based on the DISC behavioral style model first developed by William Moulton Marston in the 1920s. DISC is an acronym that denotes **D**ominance, **I**nfluence, **S**teadiness, and **C**onscientiousness—the four basic behavioral traits of healthy people. We will represent these characteristics as Eagles (D), Parrots (I), Doves (S), and Owls (C). Why use birds? Because these colorful metaphors will quickly reveal themselves as illuminating, memorable representations of the four styles.

In my first book, *Taking Flight!*, my coauthor and I introduced the birds in a fable format. This book will both reintroduce the bird styles themselves and deepen our understanding of how each operates, flourishes, and struggles in the world of work.

THE BIRDS AT A GLANCE

- An **Eagle's** primary focus is achieving results: they are decisive, direct, and action oriented. (*Dominant*)
- A **Parrot's** primary focus is social interaction: they are optimistic, fun seeking, and spontaneous. (*Influential*)
- A **Dove's** primary focus is building harmony: they are patient, sincere, and attentive. (*Steady*)
- An **Owl's** primary focus is achieving accuracy: they are detail oriented, systematic, and analytical. (*Conscientious*)

BEGIN WITH YOU

The most reliable way to understand your own style is to take a DISC profile. There are many DISC profile vendors online. To take our Velocity Birds profile, go to OrderDISC.com. Once you've discovered your DISC type, use the key above to translate your DISC results to your bird type.

In Chapter 1, we will cover a wide range of benefits heightened self-awareness activates in your life. Chapters 2 through 5 feature an in-depth analysis of each bird type, highlighting the strengths, challenges, and amusing head scratchers we experience in our workplace lives.

In Chapter 6, we will learn the art and science of birdwatching: reading a person's body language and tone of voice to identify their style combination. Chapter 7 reviews style combinations in depth, and the final chapter discusses the opportunities unleashed when we embrace the rich diversity of styles that surround us.

Taken together, these topics will give you greater insight into your professional relationships, as well as increase awareness of your own behavioral style. As we'll learn in the next chapter, this can have a critical impact on your happiness and health. Let's get started.

CHAPTER ONE

Self-Awareness: The Root of Healthy Relationships

___

"There are three things extremely hard: steel, a diamond, and to know one's self."

—BENJAMIN FRANKLIN

I recently had a conversation with a former colleague we'll call Ted who captured a core concept behind this book. After we caught up, he asked me, "Hey, Dan, I'm a nice guy, right?"

I paused. "Well, that's an interesting question. Why do you ask?"

Ted replied, "I had a 360-degree feedback report done as

part of my annual review, and it wasn't pretty. Apparently, I'm very difficult to work with. But *you* know me, Dan! I'm a nice guy, right?"

I paused for a bit and replied, "Actually, you're not. I would say that you're hardworking, hold yourself to high standards, and are very driven to succeed. But 'nice' is not how I would describe you."

Ted was frustrated. "We've known each other for years. Why haven't you ever told me that before?" he asked.

"I thought you knew," I responded. "The rest of us do."

Have you ever seen the meme of a kitten who looks into a mirror and sees a lion staring back? Ted is the opposite of this—he's a lion who looks in the mirror and sees a kitten as his reflection. This might seem funny, or you may assume Ted isn't a very bright guy. However, traditional definitions of intelligence do not apply here. Ted is, in fact, exceptionally bright. He just lacks self-awareness.

Many of us are like Ted. We look in the mirror and see something a bit different from what the rest of the world experiences. In other words, we have a skewed self-image. This is problematic, because if you don't fully understand yourself and how you interact with the world, it becomes difficult to understand why people react to you the way they do. Not understanding yourself, therefore, makes building healthy relationships more difficult.

Because Ted wasn't seeing himself clearly, he had no idea his communication style had damaged several work relationships, which led to significant performance issues with his team. Ted's group suffered from higher-than-normal staff turnover, poor communication, and an inability to execute projects on deadline. Thus, Ted's inability to build healthy relationships led to creating team dysfunction that now threatened his job.

Ted's spiral is not surprising. According to Travis Bradberry, the author of *Emotional Intelligence 2.0*, "...83 percent of people high in self-awareness are top performers and just 2 percent of bottom performers are high in self-awareness."[1]

When a person possesses high levels of self-awareness, healthy relationships can be built on a powerful foundation. Self-knowledge reveals your gifts and challenges, which enables you to better leverage the complementary skills of others. You can both pinpoint which of your behaviors annoy your colleagues and better understand why their behaviors get under your skin. As Carl Jung said, "Everything that irritates us about others can lead us to an understanding of ourselves."

---

1   Travis Bradberry and John Greaves, *Emotional Intelligence 2.0* (San Diego: Talent Smart, 2009).

THE POWER OF SOFT SKILLS

Businesses are taking notice of the importance of positive relationships at work. According to Gallup, the American economy loses more than $360 billion annually due to poor employee-manager relationships.[2] An MIT/IBM study found employees with healthy relationships generate more revenue than those with weak ties—in excess of $900 per email contact.[3] This is why many large organizations are investing in the creation of social spaces that encourage frequent social interaction. Such environments foster increased communication and stronger social bonds, the combination of which translates into overall increased productivity.

Now, let's take this a step further. A wide range of studies reveals healthy relationships are the biggest factor in determining your level of happiness. While happiness is its own reward, this state of mind releases a cascade of additional benefits.

YOUR BRAIN ON HAPPINESS

When you're happy, your brain releases serotonin, dopamine, and oxytocin. Not only do these neurotransmitters make you feel good, they also connect the learning centers of your brain, sparking creativity and innovation.

2   Shawn Achor, *The Happiness Advantage* (New York: Crown Business, 2010), 34.

3   Achor, *The Happiness Advantage*, 28.

They unleash your potential to solve problems and spot opportunities that otherwise would have been missed. Essentially, happiness makes you smarter.

In *The Happiness Advantage,* best-selling author Shawn Achor documents the startling connection between happiness and productivity. Reports Achor, "Doctors put in a positive mood before making a diagnosis show almost three times more intelligence and creativity than doctors in a neutral state, and they make accurate diagnoses 19 percent faster. Students primed to feel happy before taking math achievement tests far outperform their neutral peers. A meta-analysis of happiness research that brought together the results of over 200 scientific studies on nearly 275,000 people found that happiness leads to success in nearly every domain of our lives: marriage, health, friendship, community involvement, jobs, careers, and business."[4]

In addition to boosting happiness and productivity, positive relationships can also impact your health. A recently published report on the Harvard Study of Adult Development tracked more than six hundred people over the course of *seventy-five years* to determine what factors play into a long and healthy life.[5] Most of the participants

---

4   Achor, *The Happiness Advantage,* 15.

5   Christina Stiehl, "The Best Path to a Long Life Has Nothing to Do with Diet or Exercise," *Thrillist,* January 23, 2017.

are now in their eighties and nineties. Over the course of their lifetimes, researchers identified critical patterns that appear in the happiest and healthiest subjects. The study's leader, Dr. Robert Waldinger, reports the following: "Relationships are super important. They're right up there alongside not smoking, exercise, diet, not abusing drugs...We begin to realize that...somehow the number and quality of relationships you have actually gets into your body and makes a difference."

Not surprisingly, negative relationships significantly impact your health as well. Dr. Waldinger continues, "People who have bad relationships, who have very stressful lives without the ability to calm down, are chronically in a kind of low-level fight-or-flight response, and that changes your body chemistry." According to the report, high levels of stress hormones can create a state of chronic inflammation, a precursor to heart disease and strokes.

A fifteen-year study found employees who had a difficult relationship with their boss were 30 percent more likely to suffer from coronary heart disease.[6]

A Tel Aviv University study published in the *Wall Street Journal* reported the following: "The number of hours a person spent at the office didn't affect his or her longevity. Instead, the factor most closely linked to health was the

6   Achor, *The Happiness Advantage*, 33.

support of coworkers: Less-kind colleagues were associated with a higher risk of dying...and the magnitude of the effect is unsettling. According to the data, middle-age workers with poor social support in the workplace were 2.4 times more likely to die during the study."[7]

The bottom line: not only are good relationships the key to happiness and productivity, but they also have the power to lengthen or shorten your life. Happily, the ability to improve nearly every relationship is well within your reach, because the formula to success begins with self-awareness.

SUCCESS FORMULA

SELF-AWARENESS
PRODUCTIVITY
RELATIONSHIPS
HAPPINESS

---

7   Jonah Lehrer, "Your Co-Workers Might Be Killing You," *Wall Street Journal*, August 20, 2011.

IT'S ALL ABOUT PERCEPTION

"But wait," you say, "I can't change my boss's obnoxious personality!" True, but you do have near complete control over how you *choose* to perceive his behavior and, therefore, the impact it has on your life. All it takes is a shift in perception to see that what you think is a wall (a stressful relationship) is actually a door. Understanding *why* people say and do the things they do depersonalizes difficult situations, handing you multiple keys to enter into a much more positive dynamic that reduces your stress. It's not hard to do. This book will demystify why you click with some and clash with others, enabling you to achieve the biggest driver of happiness—healthier relationships.

I once coached a manager—let's call her Jackie—who was convinced her boss was sexist. She responded to him by pretending not to notice, digging in and working harder. Over time, however, their toxic dynamic diminished her vitality and significantly increased her stress. Jackie's husband offered advice on how to handle the situation, but she wasn't comfortable with his approach. This compounded the situation by creating stress in *their* relationship.

I asked Jackie, "Does your manager treat you differently than he treats men?" She said "yes" and then backtracked. "Actually, I don't really know." I asked her to spend the next two weeks intently observing her boss's behavior with both men and women. On our next call, Jackie was ecstatic. "What happened?" I asked. "He's a jerk to everybody!" she replied.

OK, he isn't sexist. Now, we dug a little deeper. Is he really a jerk, or is he just a certain behavioral type that behaves in a predictable way when under stress? First, I asked Jackie how *she* handled stress. "I become very scattered, talk too much, and eventually freak out," she replied. Given this was likely the opposite behavioral style of her boss, I then listed a number of stress behaviors that would be typical of his style: emotionally remote, condescending, sarcastic, and dismissive. "Yes!" Jackie said. "That's exactly how he is." Well, sure. That's how most people with his style behave under stress. Jackie's boss was what we call an Owl overusing his style traits.

Finally, I asked Jackie if there might be some stress in her boss's life. "Management is putting a lot of heat on us to beat last year's numbers," she responded. "That can't be fun to deal with at his level." OK, so not only has Jackie's boss been acquitted of sexism, but also, he may not even be a jerk.

This shift in Jackie's perspective significantly impacted her life. Within a month, she turned that relationship around, her outlook dramatically improved, her energy levels rose, and not surprisingly, her productivity soared—

which helped her boss meet his goals. Ironically, she also discovered her husband and boss shared the same Owl personality type! By resolving the issue with her boss, Jackie now saw her husband in a whole new light, which improved that relationship as well.

WHY THIS MATTERS

As Jackie realized, there's a human tendency to interpret people problems we don't understand with a negative explanation. We create narratives about others that often have nothing to do with reality and then seek evidence that reinforces our pet narrative. Not only is this habit not particularly fair, but it's also self-sabotaging. The more I decide you're not someone I like or respect, the more stressed I become when interacting with you, which puts my body into duress, suppressing my own health and well-being.

Once we understand the bird styles of Eagles, Parrots, Doves, and Owls, we can stop creating delusions that give us permission to dislike people. Instead, we become curious about style differences, recognize other perspectives as valuable, and leverage each other for a more powerful shared result. As Abraham Lincoln said, "I don't like that man. I'm going to have to get to know him better."

MATCH THE MOMENT, NOT THE MIRROR

Contrary to popular belief, the biggest reason we have unhealthy relationships isn't because we're surrounded by jerks who are out to get us. It's because we misunderstand our differences. The way in which we see the world, set expectations, and react to difficult situations is so natural, and so instinctive, we have to make a conscious effort to step back and consider how somebody else could possibly react differently to the same set of circumstances.

To create a true competitive advantage, match the moment, not the mirror. Respect your cohort's differences and lean in their direction. One of the most powerful applications of this material is sharpening your ability to peer past somebody's difficult behavior and recognize their intentions from a predictable style perspective. By understanding the roots of others' behavior and adapting your own actions to match them, you can clear away their resistance. Collaboration becomes easier.

Matching the moment does not mean reinventing your personality, nor does it suggest you become phony. Leaning in the direction of others expands your own behavioral repertoire and helps you avoid what world-renowned executive coach Marshall Goldsmith calls an "obsessive need to be me," which means adhering to a limited self-perception of who you are. Instead, be expansive in your vision of who you *can* be by flexing to the right style at the right time. This enables everyone's best contributions to shine for the betterment of all.

When "the moment" requires you to behave outside of your natural style, it will feel awkward. That's good. Like growing pains, that sensation means you're developing new muscles. With practice, you will be able to address similar situations with grace and confidence.

By adjusting your behavior toward the styles of others, you become a catalyst in facilitating their greatest contributions, which is the essence of leadership. Leadership is not a title; it's a decision. No matter where you are in your career, you can think and act like a leader by facilitating the genius of other people.

In the next section, we'll walk through each of the bird types—Eagle, Parrot, Dove, and Owl—and see the world from each perspective, so we don't fall into a trap so concisely expressed by George Carlin: "Everyone driving slower than you is an idiot. Everyone driving faster than you is a maniac."

CHAPTER TWO

Eagles

EAGLE BASICS: RESULTS ORIENTED, DIRECT, DECISIVE

KEYWORDS THAT CAPTURE EAGLES' ATTENTION:

- Win, powerful, big, best, greatest, fast, quick, challenge, obstacle, productive, momentum, complete, simple, achieved
- *Avoid: Maybe, try, perhaps*

John Chambers is the executive chairman and former CEO of Cisco, a $40 billion technology Goliath. A few years ago, Chambers went on a business trip to Israel to visit Cisco's newest R&D center. While there, he met with the local employees to host a Q&A town hall.

Culturally, Israel exhibits many Eagle traits: assertive,

direct, competitive, and intense. I often joke that if you go shopping for groceries in Tel Aviv, and you don't pack some Eagle attitude for the trip, you're not coming home with food.

Were Chambers to have hosted this session at one of Cisco's American facilities, he would have been greeted with great deference—like a conquering emperor. In Israel, Chambers went onstage only to find himself barraged by aggressive demands and questions. *We can take on more important projects. Why aren't we doing this? Have you thought about giving us more profitable work?*

Chambers was stunned, but it didn't take long for the CEO to happily adjust. "These people are going to do great things!" he later remarked to a colleague. If these employees could be fearless in challenging their CEO, it meant they wouldn't settle for anything less than the best for themselves. They were in it to *win*.

For Eagles, the road to happiness is lined with achievements, which requires consistently setting and achieving goals: personal goals, professional goals, easy-to-achieve goals, ambitious goals, ludicrous goals. This style is instinctively competitive in both their personal and professional life. An Eagle child will *thirst* to win every game. The Eagle employee you just hired will immediately set his or her sights on advancing quickly through your organization and bristle with frustration if his or her achievements don't result in tangible growth. For Eagles, if you don't have a target, you're dawdling through life. Eagle styles instinctively believe thinking big and chasing victory leads to a life worth living.

RECOGNIZING THE EAGLE STYLE

Eagles display hallmark behaviors that will tip you off to their bird type, which we will cover in the following pages. Also important is understanding the intent behind these behaviors. This is challenging when confronted with Eagle energy in real time—at the water cooler, when you're under stress, while they're giving you "feedback," or while delegating a task. In these moments, their energy and tone may rub you the wrong way, but understanding the Eagle perspective and intent may save you the trouble of being put off in the first place.

EAGLE COMMUNICATION

Eagles are wired for brevity. If a thought can be expressed quickly, why waste time with unnecessary elaboration? Eagles don't engage in conversation so much as look for the first opportunity to cut to the chase and move on. This leads other styles to believe that Eagles are not the sharpest tool in the shed. Eagles both know this and don't care. They've got bigger goals to pursue than impressing coworkers with the sound of their own voice. I once coached an Eagle executive who received feedback that his terseness in meetings suggested he either didn't have much to offer or didn't want to be there.

Here's how our conversation unfolded:

Dan: "So what do you think about this feedback?"

Exec: "These meetings are either unnecessary or poorly run."

Dan: "Why not fix them, then?"

Exec: "I am."

Dan: "How?"

Exec: "By asking the questions that matter most in a tone that says I'm not interested in wasting time. My behavior is intentional. If I can sum up where we're going in two minutes, they shouldn't need another ten to arrive at the same place."

This Eagle style didn't see himself as being blunt or abrupt. He was simply being efficient on his boss's dime. That's not rude; it's considerate. Generally speaking, this style of communication is not a reflection of the Eagle's feelings about you. Yet, other styles tend to assume something is wrong. "Why does he talk to me that way? Is he upset with me?" As an Eagle would say, ruminating about other people's potential feelings is a waste of time. If an Eagle has something to say, he'll simply say it. This style will be just as direct with the people they love most in their personal lives as they are with you.

DECISIVENESS

One way to gain insight into why people say and do the things they do is to ask yourself what keeps them up at night. The answer for Eagles is *progress*. *Are we performing at a high enough level? Are we missing an opportunity? Are we going to win?* Here's what Eagles are not worrying about: mistakes, challenges, setbacks, obstacles—yours or their own. To an Eagle, these realities are called life, so bring it on!

Accordingly, Eagles would rather decisively make a mistake than endlessly circle a situation waiting for perfect circumstances to crystalize before acting. What's more, repeated failure does *not* slow their pace. To Eagles, mistakes make you smarter, so you might as well make them often but never twice. This style isn't interested in theoretical constructs that merely live in someone's mind. Eagles enjoy grappling with the world in real time—filled with surprises and shifting realities. However, this "trusting your gut" approach to decision making often comes across as reckless, impulsive, and arrogant to other styles.

THE QUEST FOR CLARITY

Clarity is the Eagle's holy grail, and that applies to either good news or bad. As such, ambiguity is the enemy. Let's say, for example, that a Parrot—a personality type best known for optimism and personal connection—returns from a sales meeting and debriefs with his Eagle manager.

"How did it go?" the Eagle asks.

"It went very well!" the Parrot responds. "We had a great lunch, and it turns out our families live in the same town. We have so much in common!"

"OK," the Eagle responds, "but did he like the product?"

"Oh, we didn't get to that today." The Parrot shrugs.

When a colleague is over-the-top happy, the Eagle thinks to himself, *What have you accomplished to justify that level of happiness?* This style wants definitive proof that the prospect is at least interested in what is being offered. Not confirming a basic level of interest means the situation is no clearer now than before they had lunch.

Unimpressed, the Eagle sales manager says to himself, "Wasted opportunity."

WHAT EAGLES CAN TEACH US

Eagles trust their intuition and are not afraid to boldly place their bets while others waver. For our purposes, we'll define intuition as passive pattern recognition that accumulates subconsciously over a lifetime, is triggered by an event in the world, and then presents itself as an inspiration or a "gut" decision. Intuition isn't voodoo or magical thinking; it's a subtle form of deep recognition around what is possible.

SINK OR SWIM

Shortly after accepting the job as CEO of a $300 million manufacturing company, Stuart recognized a core problem. The leadership team he inherited had created a culture of complacency. Important initiatives lacked basic accountabilities such as budget constraints and milestone reviews, employees worked not a minute longer than eight hours a day, and executives were either late to meetings or on their phones during presentations.

Within two weeks, Stuart had seen enough. He scheduled an off-site leadership team summit to take place *over the weekend* and opened the event with a clear review of the company's deteriorating financial performance. He then connected dots that were uncomfortable for attendees to hear: "If this leadership team clocks out at 5:00 p.m., then why should employees behave any differently? If we don't possess clarity around core priorities, detailed execution plans to achieve them, and a culture of disciplined flexibility to adjust on the fly, how can we be successful? The answer is that we won't be successful. We will fail, and you will no longer be here." He then set a revenue goal for the coming year that represented a significant stretch of the imagination for the team. "We're either going to figure this out together or fail together. Which team do you want to be on?"

Over the ensuing months, the group hyperfocused on what success required while three leaders were fired due to poor performance. One year later, the company hit its stretch revenue goals.

This is what Eagle energy looks like: sink or swim. For other styles, the pressure to deliver without knowing exactly *how* goals will be achieved is highly stressful. In defense of their own insecurities, they will blame the Eagle's "arrogance" and "recklessness" for creating an environment of fear.

The Eagle sees it differently. Fear is a personal choice in response to an environment predicated on performance.

For those who fully apply themselves, performance will lift the team higher than they have ever experienced before. Although Eagles don't generally make the best confidants to emotionally confide in, they can inspire tremendous confidence in their people. When an Eagle looks you in the eye and says, "I believe in you, and you're going to succeed," you will likely respond with more intensity and perseverance than you knew you possessed.

In reality, Eagle intuitive energy combines humility with confidence. Their inner voice is saying, "I don't know *how* we're going to do this, but if I surround myself with partners who will relentlessly engage, solutions will be found. Let's win."

CONFLICT: THE HIDDEN GENIUS OF EAGLES

The hidden genius of Eagles lies in their ability to embrace candid conversations.

In my seminars, I often ask the group, "Eagles, how do you feel about conflict?"

"Bring it on!" Eagles shout back at the stage without hesitation.

I turn to the other styles assembled and ask, "What's with these people anyway?"

A room full of Parrots, Doves, and Owls all smile and give me a look that says, "Those Eagles are crazy." We probably all have that boss or coworker who relishes flying into the fray with an intensity that shocks others into silence. Most of us interpret this as naked aggression, arrogance, or competitiveness taken too far.

Ask an Eagle why they relish verbal combat, and they'll say because that's how problems get solved. Underneath, however, lies a deeper explanation—Eagles don't take conflict personally.

Stop for a moment and think about how freeing that is. If it's not personal, then what's the problem? I'm not going to be wounded, and neither are you. We're just going to plow our way through our opposing views until we arrive at the best idea or solution. No big deal, and we all win. This is why two Eagles can rip each other's heads off and then go have lunch together. It's simply not personal.

Contrary to what other styles inevitably think, Eagle styles don't need to be right, but they do need to win. There's a difference. Being "right" represents a personal need. "Winning" impacts the whole team in a positive way. If you can get an Eagle to see that your idea will lead to a victory, she will drop her point of view. The pathway to get there, however, requires a vigorous debate in the arena of results—one that Eagles find energizing.

Here's an example of why other styles could use a dose of Eagle conviction. Jane is an Eagle and George is a Dove—a style known for caution and patient deliberation. Jane and George have different opinions about the best way to approach a potential client. Jane states her case with confidence and can't wait to hear George's response. In fact, she expects him to respond with equal conviction. However, George is frozen by the intensity of the moment. He chooses a conciliatory response, asks to think about it a bit more, and walks out of the room thinking, She won't listen to me or respect my point of view. As he exits, Jane shrugs and thinks, I guess he didn't believe in his own idea very much. She carries on with her day satisfied the best solution won.

Had George fully engaged himself, however, they might have had a meeting of the minds or at least understood each other's point of view. Instead, he's now frustrated, and Jane has no idea their relationship is damaged. Why? Because what a Dove calls a conflict, an Eagle calls a conversation.

Non-Eagle styles often equate passionate debate with a personal attack, but letting go of this association has the potential to be liberating. For Eagles, it's about the task at hand, not the person. For non-Eagles like George, depersonalizing these situations would likely lead to healthier communication.

WHAT WE CAN TEACH EAGLES

Eagles are often mischaracterized as having big egos, the kind of people who make everything about themselves. However, it's also common to hear the following from Eagle coworkers and direct reports: "I wasn't looking forward to working with him because of his reputation, but once you get to know the guy, he's actually great." That's right. Once you get to know Eagles, their reputation for arrogance and indifference toward other people dies on the vine, because it's simply not true. However, Eagles should be aware that toning down some of their behaviors can go a long way toward preventing this stereotype from forming in the first place.

THE RIPPLE EFFECTS OF EAGLE DIRECTNESS

As you've seen, Eagles will cut to the chase, because they believe brevity combined with clarity leads to faster results, and this is true in many workplace scenarios. However, this one- communication-style-fits-all approach often backfires.

For example, declarative speech signals to a Dove that the Eagle is not open to their ideas. The result? The Dove will likely slow down in order to sort out how they really feel about the situation.

An unequivocal tone raises red flags in an Owl's mind:

"Does he have all the data? Has he thought this through? Does he understand the impact this will have down the line?" Owls will eventually question the competence of an Eagle who doesn't communicate with consistent, analytical rigor.

Parrots will smile in response to an Eagle's bluntness, but they would much prefer a collaborative approach that enables their ideas to be heard.

So, this is highly ironic. Eagles sincerely want colleagues to experience the thrill of higher productivity, yet their direct style can decrease a Dove's commitment, short-circuit an Owl's critical-thinking process, and diminish a Parrot's enthusiasm.

What if our Eagle friend reduced his directness by, say, 20 percent? With this minor adjustment that requires only a little self-awareness, our Eagle friend can surface the best thinking and efforts of his Parrot, Dove, and Owl colleagues.

WORKING WITH AN EAGLE

Let's crack the code on what Eagles do that stresses out other styles, because once a behavior is predictable, you can choose to not let it bug you and deploy a strategy that improves the relationship.

FOCUS ON THE BOTTOM LINE

Do you have a coworker who listens with an invisible stop-watch in her hand, ticking away? When you talk, does she glance at her phone, get fidgety, or otherwise signal for you to hurry up? Chances are she's an Eagle, and this behavior stems from a very different place than you might guess.

Eagles view listening as a prelude to action. The quicker you can provide clarity around what you need, the faster the Eagle can summon their problem-solving abilities to help you.

Therefore, what is perceived as rude, dismissive behavior is typically nothing more than a clumsy Eagle style attempt to be helpful. So the next time an Eagle gives you that "hurry up" vibe, choose to not be offended. Simply tell them what you need. Clarity, as always with this style, is king.

Explaining how Eagles listen to other people at Velocity seminars is one of my favorite experiences. Inevitably, there's a collective moment of realization that never gets old. "*Oh,*" the non-Eagles in the audience breathe, "my boss *isn't* an asshole!" The Eagles in the room are right with them. "Yeah!" they chime in. "We just want to get things done." I once had an Eagle turn to the rest of the group and say with a big smile, "But if calling me that will help you get the job done, go for it!"

Accordingly, never start a conversation with an Eagle by saying, "I just need forty-five minutes of your time," or "I've got a ten-page spreadsheet for you to review." (I'm talking to you, analytical Owls.) *Do* start a conversation by stating a problem or objective. For example, if you walk into an Eagle's office and say, "You're about to lose," you will have their complete attention.

Also, understand when an Eagle answers your concerns with what seems to be a brief or undetailed reply, it's not a sign of dismissing either the issue or your feelings. She will simply give you the information necessary to take action and trust you are smart enough to figure out the rest by yourself. For this style, that's a sign of respect.

EAGLES WERE BORN RIGHT—JUST ASK THEM

An Eagle's default position is that they're right. As we talked about earlier, they don't *need* to be right—what they need is to win—but they do *assume* they're right. Because this is essentially a genetic predisposition, you might as well get over it.

EAGLES' DELEGATION STYLE

Eagles value autonomy for themselves and are happy to provide latitude to others who have the guts to be proactive. An Eagle manager will assume that if her people are given the authority to make their own mistakes, they will be more successful in the long run. In addition, Eagles have little patience for bureaucracy and will swing a machete to any red tape that gets in their way.

Not surprisingly, when Eagles delegate work, they do so without a lot of instruction. This is often stressful for other behavioral types who want more in-depth discussion and direction. A Dove, for example, might feel as though she's nothing more than a cog in the wheel without an in-depth review of expectations. An Owl looks for detailed structure as a sign of effective planning. By contrast, an Eagle views her hands-off approach as a sign of confidence and trust in the people she works with.

THE STRESSED-OUT EAGLE

One of the more amusing conversations I have with Eagle clients is the stress test. "Can people tell when you're stressed out?" I ask. "Of course not," the Eagle scoffs. Then, I ask his direct reports, and they laugh. One Owl remarked, "The purple vein that pops from the center of his forehead is a clue."

Typically, an Eagle under stress will act out with high intensity, a harsh tone, and vocal pyrotechnics. Then, like a Texas thunderstorm, it's gone. Eagles rarely incubate long-term grudges against other people, and holding on to yesterday's stress would simply slow them down today.

Under severe duress, however, Eagles will react in the complete opposite direction. They'll go silent and check out. This is rare, because Eagles are hands-on—they want to be in the game in order to influence events and win. If an Eagle takes himself *out* of the game, that's a sign of higher-than-normal stress.

DEALING WITH A STRESSED-OUT EAGLE

Remember, conflict is nothing more than a route to a solution for this style. Although bearing the brunt of Eagle wrath is not fun, the best course of action is to let them vent and let it roll off your shoulders. Within ten minutes, she'll have moved on. All the better if you can too.

If you find yourself in the Eagle's line of fire, be task oriented. This is especially true if the problem is a mistake you made. Don't talk about feelings; instead, focus on the steps you're going to take to resolve the issue. Fully own your role and outline what you learned so it won't happen again. Do this in a matter-of-fact tone, and the Eagle will likely trust you *more* than before you messed up. Remember, Eagles aren't up at night worried about your mistakes, but how you handle adversity is a major indicator of whether an Eagle can count on you.

Likewise, if you're the one under stress, tell your Eagle *specifically* what you need. An Eagle will not be very useful as an emotional sounding board, but he will be happy to help you solve the problem.

QUICK TIPS FOR INFLUENCING AN EAGLE

- Be brief.
- Be authentic.
- Focus on big-picture objectives.
- Use action-oriented language and declarative sentences.
- Open with a problem that his or her participation can help solve.
- Keep your energy high, whether that means speaking or walking quickly.
- Watch for darting eyes and watch checking to determine when an Eagle wants to wrap it up.
- Avoid ambiguity.
- Sit or stand straight, make eye contact, and speak with confidence.

THE EAGLE MANAGER

The chances are high that you have worked for Eagle managers or leaders. Their confidence and driving ambition makes this style the most likely to rise into management roles.

Eagle managers are task focused and goal oriented. Their central organizing focus is to achieve results each and every day. As such, an Eagle manager will not give you an "A" for effort. This style evaluates others based on achievement, not feelings. This is difficult for other styles who seek appreciation for the hard work they provide, but Eagles already expect you to work hard. This manager style expects colleagues to be proactive problem solvers and communicate issues only after many approaches have already been tried.

Eagle managers take tremendous pride in team performance and will mentor those who show promise. Their task focus and terse communication style should not be misconstrued as being impersonal. They care about people a great deal—through the prism of performance and results. Finally, this style appreciates candid communication from others. It's much better to address issues up front than hold back for fear of a negative reaction.

LEADERSHIP PRIORITIES

- **Action oriented:** Focuses on progress through taking action
- **Clear communication:** Prioritizes brevity and clarity
- **Confidence:** Utilizes self-assurance and grand visions to inspire others
- **Risk taking:** Will stretch what is possible to achieve a competitive advantage

BIRD BY BIRD
EAGLES WORKING WITH PARROTS

Parrots and Eagles have a lot in common. They are fellow adventurers, risk takers, and general go-getters. They are both extroverts who can be gregarious in social situations. However, an Eagle's intensity around task completion can strike Parrots as disconnecting and unfriendly. The following are some tips for Eagles working with Parrots.

1. **Open with informalities.** Parrots enjoy connecting with the person behind the colleague or manager. When this style gets comfortable emotionally, they'll give you their best thinking.
2. **Encourage their input.** Parrots love to collaborate and brainstorm. Encourage them to come up with different approaches for completing projects through dialogue. The more interested they are in what they're doing, the more that task will be prioritized.
3. **Anticipate a lack of structure in execution.** Parrots

are not natural planners. Respectfully offer to help them organize project time lines.

4. **Address feelings, not just tasks.** This style is emotionally attuned to others. They care about how other people feel and seek personal approval. Address how you feel about what they're doing, and Parrots will respond.

5. **Focus on the positive.** When giving constructive feedback, emphasize their strengths and opportunities. Parrots will adjust their behavior and thinking from a place of positivity.

EAGLES WORKING WITH DOVES

These two styles are a study in contrasting approaches. Eagles speak their gut, and Doves weigh the consequences of speech before speaking. From the Dove's perspective, the Eagle's abrupt, forceful communication style is both rude and needlessly confrontational. Eagles see it differently: having to walk on eggshells to avoid the *appearance* of conflict is like living in a padded cell.

On the considerable plus side, Eagles respect Doves' strong work ethic. Doves are often drawn to Eagles' clarity of direction and confidence. Together, Eagles and Doves make a powerful team.

When working with Doves, Eagles should keep the following in mind:

1. **Slow it down.** Rapid communication of multiple execution objectives will *not* lead to a more efficient outcome. Deliver your message with calm, methodical, deliberateness, and Doves will be primed to execute.

2. **Beyond the worker.** This style wants to be appreciated for who they are, not just the role they play. Engage in conversation that is more personal in nature. Ask about their hobbies and their family. Build an authentic relationship that takes interest in the whole person.

3. **Delegate thoughtfully.** When assigning projects, give the Dove style time to absorb what the task represents through a patient conversation. How will this project impact the team, a customer, or the organization itself? What would be the surest path to the result desired?

4. **Lower your intensity.** A loud, commanding tone will slow down the adoption rate of your ideas with this style. Intensity encourages both Doves and Owls to react with skepticism, because it suggests emotion has replaced thoughtfulness in your decision making.

5. **Solicit their ideas.** Do not assume that a quiet Dove signals that they agree with you. This style is humble by nature. Encourage Doves to share their thoughts early and often, or you may be missing out on a great idea.

EAGLES WORKING WITH OWLS

Eagles and Owls share a task-oriented perspective, focusing on what needs to be accomplished. Their contrast in styles revolves around *how* they arrive at the same place. Eagles will survey the situation at a high level; Owls will dig deep into the details. Eagles will often make a quick gut decision based on past experience/intuition; Owls will painstakingly arrive at a decision after careful analysis.

When working with Owls, Eagles should keep the following in mind:

1. **Analysis is key.** Communicate the reasoning behind your decision. Owls look for a consistent, logical rationale as the backbone of decision making.
2. **Drop the intensity.** Avoid speaking in a loud and aggressive tone of voice. Like with Doves, Owls interpret emotional communication as representing a lack of rigor in arriving at a point of view. High levels of emotion only bring out an Owl's skepticism.
3. **Avoid aggressive deadlines.** Forcing an Owl to complete projects without the requisite time and resources to ensure high-quality results is a significant stressor for this style. This leads to analysis paralysis on how to move forward when optimal results are not likely to be realized.
4. **Ask questions.** Give the Owl style room to think in a conversation with you by converting directives into

questions. For example, "We should do this," becomes "Would it make sense for us to do this?" This approach mirrors how they actually think and will result in better conversations.

5. **Be prepared.** Winging it is not impressive to Owls. Come prepared to discuss your subject in depth, with materials to share and having formulated a structured point of view.

TOP TEN CONSIDERATIONS FOR EAGLES

- **Directness.** Overusing this approach will decrease the commitment of others to your point of view.
- **Fast pace.** Ease up. Fully listening to others will enable smarter solutions and improve relationships.
- **Competitiveness.** You don't need to win every conversation and dispute. This behavior weakens team spirit.
- **Ego.** Communicate how others will genuinely benefit. Otherwise, it's just about you.
- **Powerful presence.** Remember that 55 percent of all communication is physical. Be aware of your body language and be sure to offer warm smiles and a more relaxed posture.
- **Need for control.** Delegate more and allow others to be decision makers.
- **Independence.** Involve others in decision making. Collaboration will both improve your own effectiveness and develop the people around you.
- **Accurate expectations.** Appreciate that others are not as intensely task oriented.
- **Conviction.** Overconfidence is often perceived as arrogance, which weakens your case.
- **Self-importance.** Yours is not the only agenda. Respect where others are coming from.

CHAPTER THREE

Parrots

PARROT BASICS: FUN, SOCIAL, OPTIMISTIC, SPONTANEOUS

KEYWORDS THAT CAPTURE PARROTS' ATTENTION:

· Fresh, fantastic, opportunity, fun, different, cool, hilarious, exciting, unique, new, interesting, innovative, big, what if
· Avoid: *Perfecting, systems, fine print*

I once worked with a Parrot executive (we'll call him Peter), who was promoted to CEO of a large organization because of his exceptional business development skills. Through genuine charisma and a subject matter expert's grasp of his industry, Peter could effortlessly build powerful relationships and inspire confidence with potential clients, strategic partners, and investors. He also genuinely cared about his team and strived to create a positive, healthy culture where everyone could both contribute to the organization and grow their careers as a result.

However, with those Parrot strengths came Parrot challenges. For starters, Peter suffered from shiny object syndrome, meaning, whatever captured his attention had his FULL attention, until the next shiny object appeared. While meetings were never boring with Peter in the room, he would often respond to questions by veering creatively in multiple streams of consciousness. The team would play follow the bouncing ball for an hour, and then Peter would leave. Confusion ensued.

After a few months on the job, the leadership team noticed something important about their CEO's decision making: whomever spoke to Peter last had the most influence. This created competition over who had the best access to the boss as opposed to who had the best ideas.

Finally, like most Parrots, Peter had a significant need to be liked. He smoothed over potential conflicts by simply telling people what they wanted to hear to achieve a short-term positive connection. That inevitably led to disappointment and frustration given that no one person, even a CEO, can make everyone happy.

Luckily for Peter, he's got great self-awareness and a Parrot's sense of humor. He knows what his challenges are and works on himself to become a great leader.

PARROTS LIVE FOR FUN

Parrots are friendly, warm, charming, charismatic, and most of all, fun to be around. Parrots *love* connecting and interacting and typically build large social networks. Because they have extensive interests, Parrots tend to have conversational knowledge spanning many topics, which makes for easy rapport building with a wide range of people.

Parrots bring an infusion of good energy and positive vibes to the workplace. They instinctively feel the purpose of life is to enjoy oneself in every sphere of life. While other styles find a buoyant disposition to be distracting and lacking professionalism, Parrots find it odd to have to defend fun in the first place. After all, if people are happy and getting along, they're probably working well together and being productive, which advances the company's mission and creates more success. So, what's the problem with fun?

RECOGNIZING THE PARROT STYLE

Parrots are energized by being around people and sharing what's on their minds. This style is very adept at building rapport through finding common ground. "You hiked in Alaska? My cousin did that." Your Parrot coworker will translate their social inclination into a thirst for collaboration. Parrots love to work in groups, bounce around new ideas, get positive reinforcement, and celebrate team success.

Parrots naturally build large social and professional networks, because they love meeting new people and are comfortable with acquaintance-level relationships. For example, Parrots will share details about their personal lives with coworkers much sooner than other styles. It's a shortcut to getting to know someone (if they share back) and builds familiarity.

KNOWLEDGE NETWORKING

Parrots leverage their large networks for more than just social purposes. When confronted with a difficult problem, they will likely solicit ideas from a wide range of contacts. The disparate ideas that flow back are often the source of Parrot creativity in problem solving. If you're struggling with a conundrum, turn to a Parrot coworker, and she will know someone who has an answer. Plus, she'll be *delighted* to make the connection for you. Try it.

TIME MANAGEMENT

My colleague Ken Blackwell has made the following astute observation about Parrots: "They've got only two modes of time management: now and not now." Right now, your Parrot coworker has seven files opened in his laptop taskbar and is working on all of them simultaneously. Why? Because Parrots have short attention spans; multiple tasks keep their interest high when one grows stale. While Eagles naturally gravitate toward the "top priority," Parrots will be magnetically drawn to what's most interesting to them *in that moment*. Having multiple choices keeps the moment interesting.

The reason your Parrot coworker hasn't finished the report you asked for last week is because there are more interesting to-dos that have captured her attention and your task got moved to the "not now" column. How can you influence the Parrot to deliver on your request? Explain in emotional terms how this issue is making your life more difficult. For example, you could say, "Sarah, I'm sure you have a lot on your plate, but if this isn't completed by Wednesday, the client will be upset. Then, I'll have to have an uncomfortable conversation with my boss about it." Parrots are sensitive to the feelings of others and will reprioritize in order to keep someone from being unhappy. Just make sure to show your happiness when they deliver. That's the payoff for a Parrot, and if you provide it, they will keep performing so they can relive the happy moments you provide.

WHAT PARROTS CAN TEACH US

Parrots believe in themselves, their choices, and the world around them through a combination of preternatural optimism and trusting that their intuition will point them in the right direction.

Billionaire entrepreneur Richard Branson is the personification of how intuition combined with optimism can make great things happen. After having built a thriving record company from scratch, Branson walked into a Virgin Records board meeting one day and said, "I have good news and great news. The good news is that I sold the record company. The *great* news is that now we're going to become an airline, Virgin Airlines."

Spying his toothy grin and reputation as a prankster, the audience assumed Branson was just being Branson. After all, why would a record label morph into an airline? As he began outlining the transition, however, they realized this was no joke.

One executive stood up and asked, "Mr. Branson, we're a record company. We know nothing about the airline industry. What analysis do you have that suggests we can

be successful in a world we know nothing about, especially when the airlines themselves don't know how to
make a profit?" Branson's response, "I'm glad you asked,
and here's my analysis: the same customers who buy our
records will now fly in our airplanes."

This did not inspire confidence for many in the room.

In fact, Branson had conducted years of research, although
not the quantitative type a more conscientious person
would prefer. Branson's passion for travel stemmed from
personal pride that his mother had been one of the world's
first flight attendants to cross the Atlantic in a commercial
airline. As the founder of Virgin Records, Branson trav-
eled internationally for decades, often in coach where he
could mingle with regular passengers and witness their
travel frustrations firsthand. Their experience featured
uncomfortable seats, bad lighting, terrible food, no leg-
room, late arrivals, and unpleasant service.

While his adventurous idea to start up an airline may have
been sudden and jarring to his board, the concept had
been brewing deep in Branson's mind for many years. His
intuition—which, again, we're defining as passive pattern
recognition that accumulates subconsciously over many
years—finally emerged with a burst of inspiration: "Let's
make flying fun!" Branson took an intuitive leap of faith
that the Virgin brand was powerful enough to command

premium pricing for a genuinely better travel experience. He was right. How is "fun" woven into Virgin Airlines? Check out this link to Virgin Airlines Safety Video: https://www.youtube.com/watch?v=DtyfiPIHsIg. This is what happens when Parrot energy runs the show.

OPTIMISM: THE HIDDEN GENIUS OF PARROTS

If you walk into a room full of Parrot coworkers and make the following announcement, "We're going to change everything around here," they will immediately cheer with enthusiasm before they know what the change is about. (Try this with a room full of Owls, and the response will be quite different.) Parrots equate "change" with "good" because of their innate optimism. Indeed, I once knew a wise Parrot who said, "If the bright side doesn't exist, then how come I keep finding it?"

How important is optimism to enjoying a full and healthy life? Dr. Martin Seligman, founder of the positive psychology movement and former president of the American Psychological Association, offers significant insight into the power optimism versus pessimism can have on our lives. Seligman describes these two mindsets as being rooted in contrasting explanatory styles.[8] Meaning, when something terrible happens to a pessimist, they explain the situation to themselves in a particular way while opti-

8   Martin E. P. Seligman, *Learned Optimism* (New York: Vintage Books, 1990).

mists will self-explain the same unfortunate occurrence very differently.

Let's say, for example, a pessimist's big business deal falls apart. "It's all my fault," he tells himself. "I have failed. I'm not good enough." In addition, the pessimist assumes this single situation represents a pattern. "This keeps happening to me for a reason. This is who I am and my lot in life."

When difficult circumstances befall an optimist (for our purposes, a Parrot), a very different dialogue runs through her mind. Instead of convicting herself, the Parrot figures, "Well, there were a lot of factors involved. I played a role in this, but so did market changes, our time constraints, and our lack of resources. This was difficult for many reasons." Seligman points out that this line of thinking is not an avoidance of accountability but an accurate recognition that outside realities exist and play a role in all endeavors.[9] Optimists simply expand their view and interpretation to a wider set of circumstances. Moreover, optimists believe negative situations are only temporary, not a preordained pattern destined for perpetuity. Things may not be great right now, but soon they will be.

Incredibly, the process reverses when good fortune strikes. Seligman found that when pessimists experience a big

---

9   Seligman, *Learned Optimism.*

win, they *don't* take the credit. Pessimists interpret good news as largely the product of luck and outside forces, assume it won't last long, and discount the long-term impact the pleasant surprise could have for them. *It's a fluke*, he will think with a shrug. The optimist, by contrast, owns the success. Finally, while pessimists see negative circumstances as permanent, they see positive outcomes as fleeting. As you've probably guessed by now, the opposite holds true for an optimist.

Over the course of more than thirty years of research, Seligman discovered the benefits of being an optimist go far beyond enjoying a more chipper outlook on life. Optimists recover from illness more quickly, they enjoy longer, healthier relationships, and they make more money over the course of their careers than pessimists. Overall, optimists win in the key categories of what we call "quality of life."

While Parrots are born optimists, each of the other styles can elevate the Parrot energy that dwells within. If you're not sure how, read Seligman's *Learned Optimism*, or hang out with some Parrots and observe them in the wild we call the office.

WHAT WE CAN TEACH PARROTS

Because of their "now, not now" time management

approach, Parrots can be quite disorganized and often establish a reputation for being unreliable.

A more uncomfortable problem you might encounter with Parrots is their tendency to share way too much information. Parrots are informal by nature, so relationship boundaries are often fungible. Through their desire to connect and build rapport with others, Parrots will tell you about their personal life much sooner than other styles—sometimes within minutes. A Parrot acquaintance you barely know will breezily recount what happened at happy hour last night, describe an argument with their spouse, and offer a political opinion or two, all delivered right before an important client call.

I once witnessed a Parrot tell a dinner table story about his wild high school days that featured nudity, a paddle, an upset teacher, and a crowd of people. Within the first few minutes, three people abruptly left the table, but he was too enthralled with himself to notice. Me? I stayed. He was hilarious.

Parrots assume just because they're informal, you should be too. Other examples include appearing too casual at a business meeting, speaking so loudly people down the hall can hear, or using inappropriate language. I once took a puddle jumper plane piloted by a Parrot. It was the worst flight I've ever been on, partly because of all the bumps and swerves, but mostly because the pilot hopped on the microphone and was too jovial and flippant in his tone and language. I saw my own concern reflected in the wide eyes of fellow passengers. While the pilot was having fun, we were clutching our seats for dear life.

INFLUENCING A PARROT

Coloring in your facts with experiential feelings—whether your own or someone else's—is an effective way to influence a Parrot. While this style can appreciate facts and figures on a spreadsheet for what they are, they won't resonate very deeply. What *will* sway a Parrot is a humanistic perspective. For example, instead of saying, "In 2008, I lost 23 percent of my portfolio," try, "In 2008, I really got hammered by the market." More examples follow:

INEFFECTIVE	EFFECTIVE
The project is behind schedule.	We're in trouble. Let's rescue the project!
I'm concerned about this.	I'm worried about this.
This is an interesting juncture.	We've got a big opportunity here.
We need to take a deeper dive.	Let's jump in and see what we can improve.

THE STRESSED-OUT PARROT

Parrots under stress are hard to miss. For starters, they're likely to announce, "I'm so stressed out! I've got a *million* things to do and a kid at home with a fever and…" You get the picture. Their style is, after all, a verbal one. In uncomfortable situations, Parrots will crack jokes and change the subject. Disapproval is not something Parrots like to either give or receive. Once their stress level hits their maximum threshold, however, look out. That jovial fun seeker is now yelling at you with a startling intensity.

Witnessing a stressed Parrot spinout can be a disconcerting experience, because there is such a huge gulf between their normal and stress behaviors. In addition, Parrots can weaponize their intuitive feel for others by hurling sharp observations that land and cut deep. However, after the storm passes, the Parrot will feel horrible and apologize profusely.

Common stress builders for this style are overcommitments, procrastination, and the realization they're about to let someone down. Because Parrots are often haphazard in how they organize their days, these issues can be difficult to solve, but they are also highly predictable.

HELPING THE STRESSED-OUT PARROT

For starters, give him room to voice pent-up frustrations. Next, help your Parrot colleague devise a plan. While Parrots might not like structure because it impedes creativity, they still *need* it, particularly when under stress. Help this style devise a disciplined approach to executing tasks, and they will be very grateful. Highly effective Parrots have learned the art and science of being creative within a set of parameters that keep them on track to actually deliver results.

To summarize, here are basic steps for helping a Parrot under high stress:

- Let them vent.
- Acknowledge their stress. (This does not mean you agree with them, only that you are validating their emotional state.)
- Don't take anything they say personally. (They'll apologize the next day anyway.)
- Offer a structured approach to solving the problem.
- Check that they followed through on the plan.

DELEGATING TO A PARROT

Avoid passing off a polished, detailed plan and asking the Parrot to merely execute on your behalf. This snuffs out her creativity and, with that, her ability to think. To a Parrot, being told what to do signifies you don't trust or believe in them, which significantly lowers their energy and enthusiasm for the task.

Instead, give Parrots only the broad outlines of the project. Tell them, "Here's the big picture. Within three months, we want to have a marketing strategy that hits these three segments of the population." This gives them room to come up with creative solutions. Encourage them to reach out with questions, because this ensures you are in the loop with their progress.

Admittedly, the hands-off approach above is risky, because Parrots are often poor at devising plans on their own. Establishing a healthy balance of autonomy versus structure is your biggest challenge with this style.

Incidentally, my colleague Dayna Williams has a wonderful metaphor that captures the Parrot approach to project management. In the middle of a meeting about one topic, the spirit of another subject will suddenly capture their minds, and colorful idea confetti is now tossed all over the room. What about this red idea? What about that blue idea? Wow! This is fun! Then, the Parrot leaves. Who cleans up a floor filled with ideas? The detail-oriented Owls.

FEED THEM WITH RECOGNITION

In and out of the office, Parrots seek approval and recognition. It fuels their inner drive to make a noticeable impact on the world. While other styles may find this irritating or even exhausting, the fact remains that regular acknowledgment and praise are the keys to sustaining a Parrot's commitment for your project.

QUICK TIPS FOR INFLUENCING A PARROT

- Be more informal in demeanor and dress.
- Smile. Parrots will connect with this and take it as a sign that you're open.
- Make physical contact, whether through a pat on the shoulder, warm handshake, or a hug.
- Talk a bit faster to pick up the energy.
- Speak in superlatives, such as, "awesome," "extraordinary," and "the best."
- If you're comfortable, reveal something personal about yourself.
- Begin an idea with "What if..." This invites a Parrot to freely explore their imagination.

THE PARROT MANAGER

Like Eagles, Parrots tend to delegate to others with lots of autonomy. The difference is whereas an Eagle will prioritize a firm deadline for executing projects, a Parrot manager will often be less concrete about time lines and deliverables. Because Parrots strongly dislike being micromanaged themselves, they err on the side of significant freedom when delegating to others. While Parrots see this as the gift of empowerment, Owls and Doves appreciate advanced planning and structure prior to assignments being delegated. Thus, what the Parrot calls "trusting in others," Doves and Owls call "being set up to fail."

Although it may feel a bit strange to "manage up" your

Parrot boss, book time on her calendar and be clear about your needs in this area. Your dissatisfaction will capture her attention, and she'll likely feel motivated to lean in your direction with better planning up-front.

LEADERSHIP PRIORITIES

- **Enthusiasm:** Motivates others through high optimism
- **Pioneering spirit:** Sees possibilities where others see obstacles
- **Relationship focus:** Invests in relationships that instill loyalty
- **Innovation:** Resourceful problem solver

LEADERSHIP CHALLENGES

- **Reliability:** Inconsistent attention to appointments and tasks
- **Process:** Neglects the mechanics of how the operation will work
- **Impulsiveness:** Quick to make decisions based on feelings rather than evidence
- **Follow-Through:** Drawn to the beginnings of projects, not their completion

BIRD BY BIRD
PARROTS WORKING WITH EAGLES

Parrots and Eagles are similar in many respects: both command attention from others through their high-energy demeanor and charisma, both have a talent for big-picture thinking, and both instinctively trust their intuition in decision making.

There are key differences, however, that Parrots should pay attention to when working with Eagles:

1. **Focus on tasks.** Eagles view execution as the primary driver of success. They focus on *what* needs to get done as efficiently as possible. When working with an Eagle, avoid brainstorming and hypotheticals. An Eagle expects you to have already thought those things through. Focus your language on tangible steps.

2. **Avoid discussion around feelings.** Quite frankly, Eagles don't respect decisions based on how you feel about a project or task. They are interested, however, in your opinion as it relates to task completion. Your language should reflect this through facts and analysis of concrete realities. What is your plan of action? What are the obstacles that will impede your progress? What steps will you take to overcome them? This is the language that connects with this style.

3. **Be punctual.** Parrots are often casual about punctuality. From an Eagle's perspective, that demonstrates a lack of commitment or seriousness.

4. **Cut to the chase.** While Parrots love to build rapport through shared interests in order to create an emotionally comfortable atmosphere, Eagles consider this as essentially unnecessary. Eagles value their

time through tasks, not emotional connection. Get straight to the business at hand and you will have the Eagle's attention.

5. **Don't seek emotional validation.** Parrots who crave an emotional or literal pat on the back are often put off by an Eagle's lack of effusive emotional connection. Our sincere advice: get over it. If you want a big smile and a hug, go to a fellow Parrot or Dove. *Eagles care about people through the prism of productivity.* Accept that and your relationship will improve.

PARROTS WORKING WITH DOVES

Both of these styles prioritize relationships over tasks and share a warm disposition. However, there are significant land mines Parrots should avoid when working with Doves.

1. **Rein yourself in.** As we talked about earlier, Doves are not eager to know intimate details of your personal life before significant trust has been built *over time.* Also, don't gossip in a negative way about those who are not present. What seems innocuous to you may well affect Doves at a deeper level.

2. **Slow down.** Doves are patient listeners, which Parrots often misinterpret as approval. A Parrot will burst into a Dove's office, excitedly share an idea, receive no immediate pushback, and assume that all is well. Only later will our disappointed Parrot find out that the

Dove didn't really agree with them. "Why didn't you just tell me then?" The answer is, Doves need time to think, weigh, get comfortable, and weigh some more before arriving at a conclusion.

3. **Listening.** Doves think in order to formulate speech. Parrots speak in order to formulate thoughts. This means it's hard for Parrots to stay quiet because their brains are frozen until they talk. However, speaking over a Dove sends the signal that their opinion doesn't matter as much as yours. Learn to listen patiently without speaking.

4. **Delegating.** Parrots like to delegate at a very high level and optimistically assume that the delegate will "figure it out." However, when delegating to this style, set aside at least thirty minutes to thoroughly hand off the project with clear expectations and, at minimum, the outlines of a plan.

5. **Change.** While Parrots are instantly optimistic with the idea of change, Doves take a different view. Only after the change has been evaluated from a good-for-the-group perspective will the Dove fully embrace it, and this takes time. When communicating change to this style, slow down and be thoughtful about the impact and ramifications it will have for the team.

PARROTS WORKING WITH OWLS

These two types are a study in opposites. Whereas Parrots

live for fun, Owls find overt enthusiasm distracting, even irritating. Parrots are experiential in nature; Owls are analytical in nature. Parrots know they're right when it *feels* right; Owls reject emotions as evidence of any kind (other than, perhaps, as the absence of logic).

Here are steps Parrots should take to have positive interactions with Owls that build healthy relationships:

1. **Tone down your emotions.** Owls expect dispassionate analysis in decision making. Emotional displays are quite literally a distraction. Keep your tone formal, your facial expressions limited, and your overall physicality restrained.
2. **Slow down.** Like your Dove colleagues, Owls do not appreciate being rushed into a decision. They require time to assess, analyze, and synthesize *before* making a decision. Honoring this approach will both improve your relationship and, yes, very likely improve the quality of your joint efforts.
3. **Anticipate questions.** Owls rarely accept a premise on face value. An Owl's primary tool for analysis is to ask questions. Lots of them. Questions reveal data that can then be scrutinized for accuracy. Parrots often interpret this painstaking approach as an interrogation, and as a lack of confidence in their ideas. The remedy: don't take it personally because it's not about you. It's about the accuracy or viability of the

idea itself. This is the Owl style's way of arriving at integrity.

4. **Be methodical.** This style appreciates a logical progression of ideas and tasks that culminate in a high-quality result. Focus your communication on the process itself, not just the end result.

5. **Details, details.** If you are not comfortable thoroughly explaining your perspective, the Owl style will question the logic behind your ideas. Take the time to methodically articulate the building blocks and how they fit together. This should be done patiently and without emotional flourishes.

TOP TEN CONSIDERATIONS FOR PARROTS

- **Need for approval.** Replace applause seeking with grounded self-confidence that your actions are their own reward.
- **Need for freedom.** Too much autonomy can lead to chaos. Seek structure and systems that help you keep commitments.
- **Avoidance of difficult conversations.** Candid conversations strengthen relationships. Laughing off real issues only creates bigger problems down the road.
- **Sky-high optimism.** Work on being realistic about what will actually take place, as opposed to a best-case scenario.
- **Casual demeanor.** Being too relaxed can send a message that you are not serious about your work.
- **Big-picture thinking.** Sometimes starting with the details and working toward the big picture will increase the quality of your work.
- **Instantaneous reactions.** Listen, *PAUSE*, respond. The pause enables you to compose your thoughts, instead of simply blurting them out.
- **Spontaneity.** Create a plan B so that others can feel confident you've thought things through before acting.
- **Being unconventional.** Appreciate the value of rules and structure.
- **Shiny object syndrome.** Prioritize based on what is most important, *not* what's most interesting or fun.

CHAPTER FOUR

Doves

—

DOVE BASICS: HARMONIOUS, PATIENT, LOYAL, ATTENTIVE

KEYWORDS THAT CAPTURE DOVES' ATTENTION:

- Guaranteed, solid, user friendly, time saving, steady, predictable, thoughtful, meaningful, connected, holistic, gradual, patient, thorough, complete
- *Avoid: Right now, conflict, bold action*

As the supervisor of eight project managers at a pharmaceutical company, Lauren is a quintessential Dove in action. Her primary task is to ensure her followers have the resources necessary to fulfill their responsibilities. Based on her bird style, this role fits Lauren like a glove—she gets paid to create a comfortable environment and to build relationships with her tight-knit team.

In many ways, Lauren is the kind of manager most people would enjoy. She puts a lot of energy into creating the best work environment possible. She holds regular one-on-one meetings with her staff, is genuinely invested in their work-life balance, and involves the group in important decisions, seeking a consensus whenever possible. She is very adept at building trust, and this creates a stable, calm environment for the team to fulfill their mission. These Dove traits enable Lauren to be a terrific manager.

However, she has recently come under scrutiny by the head of IT, whose team works closely with her department. He's concerned about what he perceives as Lauren's reluctance to hold poor performers accountable and a lack of urgency around deadlines.

Lauren now finds herself in her *least* favorite scenario in business and in life—conflict. She is faced with delivering a difficult message to her team, confronting her own role in creating this perception, and having some less-than-pleasant conversations with the head of IT.

HARMONY SEEKERS

Doves seek a sustained state of harmony among people. When a group operates in harmony, the work gets done efficiently without drama or conflict, and everyone is comfortable in their role. For Doves, this represents the optimal state for sustained success.

HIGHLY PATIENT

I'm willing to bet the most patient people in your life are Doves. They effortlessly play the role of engaged audience no matter who has the stage, which is particularly attractive to effervescent Parrots who love to talk. Combined with their high levels of agreeableness, this patience equips Doves with a sympathetic, likable, comfortable presence. Not surprisingly, this is both a great asset to Doves and can also work against them. We'll dive into both shortly.

SOFT-SPOKEN

Doves tend to be soft-spoken in their demeanor, but this should not be interpreted as a lack of resolve. Once a Dove makes a commitment, they will stubbornly pursue its completion no matter what obstacles present themselves. This is the strong, silent type.

The shadow side of a Dove's agreeable nature is they often refrain from voicing their opinion even if they disagree with what is transpiring. For example, if a Dove has a great idea that is at odds with what the group collectively thinks, they probably won't share it for fear of being disruptive.

PROCESSES AND SYSTEMS

Like their Owl colleagues, Doves appreciate environments built on established systems and processes that create predictability and stability. For Doves, the alternative to structure is chaos, which only leads to stress and conflict.

TIME MANAGEMENT

While Eagles and Parrots can ricochet from one project to the next without hesitation, Doves prefer a deliberate and commitment-oriented approach to managing their time. In an ideal environment, they commit to a project, create a plan, methodically execute each stage, deliver the finished result, and only then make another commitment. In accounting terms, this single-minded approach is often called first in, first out (FIFO). The real world, however, requires Doves to juggle multiple priorities with varying degrees of difficulty versus competence, clarity versus ambiguity of the tasks involved, and high versus low consequences if deadlines are missed. These dynamic forces are often stressful for this style, whose primary goal is to fully deliver on each of their commitments. Their solution whenever possible: FIFO.

WHAT DOVES CAN TEACH US

Listening is a critical relationship-building skill, one that is remarkably overlooked in both primary schooling and professional development training. A colleague of mine, Merrick Rosenberg, often asks groups the following: "Think about a person in your life who really listens to you. Now ask yourself, how much do you like them?" It's a great question because without fail, everyone responds they like *that* person very much. In fact, it's difficult to dislike someone who really listens to you, because that activity is a fundamental sign of respect. Now, let's consider the opposite. How easy is it to disregard or dislike a person whom we feel doesn't listen to us? Again, the universal response is obvious.

Doves are born with the gift of presence, which enables them to listen attentively. They take the time to fully understand the circumstances, emotional composition, and desires of others. This innate skill enables Doves to build deep, long-lasting relationships. In the business world, effective listening alone has the potential to surface great ideas, maximize team performance, and build powerful client relationships. The Dove's gift for listening often makes them highly effective as leaders.

THE HIDDEN GENIUS OF DOVES: THEY DON'T NEED TO BE RIGHT

In talks and training sessions given all over the world, Dove participants affirm that being the one in the room who is *right* is not important to them. Doves possess an innate understanding that the collective is smarter than the individual. This hidden genius drives Dove leaders to cultivate the intelligence of everyone on the team, creating environments in which everyone volunteers their best thinking and efforts.

WHAT WE CAN TEACH DOVES

I often have the following conversation with Doves at our seminars. First, I ask if their coworkers tend to confide in them about both their professional and personal difficulties and stresses. Without fail, they all smile and nod.

"Why do people do this?" I continue.

"Because we listen and they trust us," they respond.

"Do you actually *want* people to routinely dump their problems on you?" More smiles, but now they are shaking their heads. "Well, then, why do you let them do it?" I respond.

"We don't want to hurt anyone's feelings," they reply.

I press further. "OK, do you also withhold candid advice that would be helpful because you're worried they might be offended?" They nod.

Of course, sometimes a sympathetic ear is exactly what

a person needs. However, excessive agreeableness can cross over into avoiding the problem-solving solutions that require courage. A healthier approach is for Doves to lean a bit into Eagle mode and shift the conversation to problem resolution. "We've talked about this a few times, so I know it's really bothering you. What steps could you take that would resolve the issue?" However, this is difficult for Doves, because they are allergic to putting pressure on others. It feels like conflict to them. Essentially, Doves often underestimate the strength of their own relationships, choosing harmony over candor. Over time, this creates another stress point around establishing and maintaining boundaries.

SETTING BOUNDARIES

It probably won't come as a surprise that Doves have a difficult time establishing boundaries. They're so focused on serving others first, second, and third that they create a pattern in relationships in which the other person's wants and needs are the top priority. Once this dynamic is established, it's very difficult to backtrack and establish healthy balance. This is compounded by the Doves' strong reluctance to not "burden" others with their own needs, no matter how much stress they're under.

I once coached a project manager we'll call Dora, who had a high-intensity Dove style. Talented and very hardworking, Dora had built a wonderful reputation in her department as a strong contributor and key leader of the group. Eventually and predictably, she created a dynamic where she couldn't get her own work done because others' requests for help had reached an unsustainable level. Averaging fifty to sixty hours a week at the office left Dora both exhausted and unable to properly meet the needs of her family that included two small children.

Her way out was both easy to diagnose and gut wrenching for her to execute. She needed to start saying "No" out loud. It took a while, but Dora gradually developed the ability to draw clear boundaries and remain very helpful to others while balancing her own needs both professionally and personally.

Essentially, she learned to flex to Eagle energy and request (or demand) greater accountability from those around her. Dora feared this approach would offend her colleagues. To her surprise and relief, their reaction was uniformly positive. Once Dora got comfortable with creating boundaries, she got on a roll, establishing clear expectations with every aspect of her professional life. This enabled her to balance her work and personal lives, which benefited not only herself but also the people she cared about in both spheres of her life.

WORKING WITH A DOVE

While we all have memories, Doves have memory museums. Here's how this works. Five years ago, you said something to a Dove they didn't like. They framed the moment and hung it on a wall somewhere in their minds, where it will remain for viewing, pretty much forever.

This emotional attachment to the past can lead to grudges being built over an extended period without your awareness. Because Doves typically avoid talking about difficult issues up-front, their discontent will often manifest itself in a passive-aggressive way. For example, let's say you're a manager who has decided to implement a significant change with the team. You've noticed that Kyle the Dove, who is always a team player, has been less productive of late. He's not openly complaining, but he *is* asking a lot more questions than you would expect, given that he signed off on this new direction some time ago. Now, you hear rumblings that Kyle has prioritized other initiatives over this project and is voicing concerns to both coworkers and colleagues outside the department. "Is this *really* the right way to go?" However, you're confused. Kyle has never once expressed doubt or dissension with you. When you ask Kyle directly about the change initiatives, he sidesteps the question and says everything is fine.

We've seen this scenario play out in many organizations. Rather than coming out and saying they don't like something, Doves will quietly build a coalition of like-minded people, then orient that community toward thwarting the initiative at hand. This behavior drives Eagles crazy. "If you weren't happy, then why didn't you say so in the beginning?" Even worse, when a Dove does speak up after the fact, the information they had been keeping to themselves makes coworkers question whether the Dove had a hidden agenda all along.

Dealing with passive aggressiveness is difficult, because by the time you've even noticed, it's probably been building for a while. Earlier detection requires noticing a Dove's noncommittal nature. Assuming the relationship is healthy enough, initiate a heartfelt conversation to try to get to the crux of how they feel. Ultimately, you are trying to create a safe environment for their concerns.

THE STRONG, SILENT TYPE

Under stress, Doves are often quite stoic and will avoid discussing their issues with others. However, your best bet for getting a Dove to speak freely is to build a trusting relationship, which takes both time and persistence. This is not easy for Eagles and Parrots, who often don't slow down enough to build a deeper rapport with this style. In a scenario where time is of the essence, here's a workable strategy: initiate an earnest conversation with your Dove colleague about the importance of their contribution to the team. You might say something like, "If you hold back your thoughts, especially when in disagreement with me, then I'll feel that you're not making a full contribution to the team. We hired you because of your talents and perspective; please don't withhold them from us. If I'm leaning in a direction that you disagree with, I'm going to ask you to stretch a bit and discuss the issue with me before it's too late to turn back. How does that sit with you?" Another tip: avoid asking "yes" or "no" questions with Doves. This gives them an easy option to not share their true feelings. Instead, use open-ended questions that begin with *what* and *how*. This will draw them out.

Essentially, Doves often need permission to speak up. Give them the green light in a thoughtful way and they will likely respond positively.

DEALING WITH CHANGE

Doves are often reluctant to embrace change quickly, because change disrupts harmony. They will instinctively direct their thoughts toward potential cultural consequences. "How will this change impact the group? Will it be good for everyone? If not, who will suffer most?" However, smart leaders are able to position their Dove colleagues as the tip of the change spear in their organizations. How? By approaching this style early on—to give them time to acclimate—and by asking them to socialize the change to others within the group or division. Doves are great at building coalitions, because others instinctively trust their motives. Involve this style early in a change process, and they will be highly effective ambassadors for your initiative.

AVOIDING CONFLICT

Because Doves simply avoid conflict, they are likely to either step aside and watch, or actively de-escalate a situation trending in a tense direction. This can be effective in keeping the room calm, but it can also stifle another person's need to get important thoughts off their chest. In addition, excessive conflict avoidance can easily lead to groupthink. If you're in a room full of Doves, the *first* idea will likely win rather than the best. While excessive strife doesn't help business, healthy conflict ensures clarity has been achieved on all sides. This is an area most Doves need to work on to be more effective.

DELEGATING TO A DOVE

Doves prefer being delegated to in a thorough and timely manner. This includes a discussion about the specifics of the assignment, ideas for how to best go about achieving goals, how this project fits in with what they're already doing, and how it aligns with other projects within the group or organization. Doves are particularly interested in how other groups will be impacted by the outcomes they are working toward. Drawing that connection is an effective way to motivate this style. What Doves don't like are assignments tossed over the wall at them. That approach makes them feel either set up to fail or taken for granted as a mere executer of tasks.

QUICK TIPS FOR INFLUENCING A DOVE

- Slow down your pace.
- Lower the intensity and volume of your voice.
- Body language should be relaxed rather than assertive.
- Hold gentle eye contact.
- Be genuine.
- Take a sincere interest in their hobbies or family life.
- Treat the Dove like a human being, not a cog in the machine.
- Focus on the positive impact their work has on others.

THE DOVE MANAGER

In *Good to Great*, a hugely successful business book about companies that consistently outperform market expectations, author Jim Collins outlines his five levels of leadership.[10] Level 5 is the pinnacle of leadership effectiveness, and there are five primary traits:

---

10 Jim Collins, *Good to Great* (New York: Harper Business, 2011).

- Level 5 leaders are self-confident enough to set up their successors for success.
- Level 5 leaders are humble and modest.
- Level 5 leaders have "unwavering resolve."
- Level 5 leaders display a "workmanlike diligence—more plow horse than show horse."
- Level 5 leaders give credit to others for their success and take full responsibility for poor results.

Guess which style most naturally embodies each one of these level 5 leadership traits? Doves.

Dove leaders have an innate ability to build trust because they are typically not driven by selfish interests. In fact, they're more likely to sacrifice their own short-term gain for the well-being of others. I have coached hundreds of Doves and find it remarkable how consistent this trait has been regardless of other factors such as gender, age, experience, or position. My Dove business partner, Dave Fechtman, also exemplifies this quality. I can point to many instances in which he has naturally focused on the other person's benefit far before contemplating his own stake in the game. For obvious reasons, this engenders tremendous goodwill and enables Dave to build healthy strategic partnerships for our organization. Dave isn't motivated to collect personal wins; he looks to create deep, healthy relationships, and this makes him a highly effective leader.

LEADERSHIP PRIORITIES

- **Trust:** Adept at earning personal loyalty
- **Thoroughness:** Deliberate decision-making process
- **Customer focus:** Prioritizes customer needs
- **Inclusiveness:** Builds consensus for major decisions

LEADERSHIP CHALLENGES

- **Passivity:** May lack assertiveness required to address difficult issues
- **Risk taking:** May seek safety over necessary change
- **Conformity:** May follow the pack instead of lead
- **Humility:** May not display confidence and passion that inspires others

BIRD BY BIRD
DOVES WORKING WITH EAGLES

Doves and Eagles are on opposite ends of the temperament spectrum. Eagles are blunt and assertive; Doves are neither. Doves are patient in decision making and seek to create a calm predictable environment; Eagles seek the near opposite in order to stay ahead of the competition.

On the considerable plus side, Eagles respect the Dove's strong work ethic, while Doves are often drawn to the

Eagle's clarity of direction and confidence. Together, these two styles make a powerful team.

When working with Eagles, Doves should keep the following in mind:

1. **Dial up your energy.** Eagles respond well to an outwardly confident disposition. Therefore, raise your energy output—sit up straight, project your voice, speak more quickly, and make steady eye contact. This aligns to their wavelength—meaning, they are instinctively more likely to listen and consider what you have to say.

2. **Don't make it personal.** An Eagle's demeanor typically ranges from assertive to aggressive. Do not take this to mean that they are annoyed with you or disapprove of your work.

3. **Be more decisive.** Eagles would much prefer that you make a mistake and get smarter than fail to make a decision. Go down swinging.

4. **Talk about tasks, not relationships.** This style is focused on progress reports, deliverables, milestones, and deadlines. Avoid a relationship or feeling-oriented focus unless it's critical to productivity.

5. **Defend your position.** If you disagree with an Eagle, be prepared to defend your perspective with a higher level of intensity than you are accustomed to displaying. To an Eagle, if you're not willing to "go to the mat," then it must not be a very good idea.

DOVES WORKING WITH PARROTS

Doves and Parrots share a natural ease with people and relationship building. Parrots are drawn to the Dove's accepting nature but often assume they are more like their Dove coworkers than is the reality. For example, Doves are even-paced; Parrots are fast-paced. Doves prefer a small group of confidants; Parrots love the crowd. Doves look to recharge with quiet time; Parrots will fill the quiet with conversation.

When working with Parrots, Doves should keep the following in mind:

1. **Up your energy.** Parrots thrive on enthusiasm. Bring more zest to your demeanor. Smile more, speak faster, make eye contact. These body language cues will endear you to this style.
2. **Embrace possibilities.** Parrots enjoy experimenting with the new. Brainstorm with them around what would be a compelling, fresh way to approach a situation. This gets their creativity rolling and energizes them to execute.
3. **Anticipate their divided attention.** Parrots are typically working on multiple projects simultaneously. What the Parrot was excited about yesterday may be on the back burner today. Expect shifting priorities, and try not to take it personally when your project gets moved to the back of the line.

4. **Up your optimism.** Parrots default to the bright side of any situation, no matter how dire. This enables them to explore outside-the-box possibilities that would improve the situation. Don't rain on that parade.
5. **Focus on the big picture.** Ever try to put a big puzzle together without seeing the finished product first? (It's usually on the box.) Spend considerable time about the project's vision first. This gives Parrots critical context from which to place the pieces.

DOVES WORKING WITH OWLS

These two styles share a calm, even-paced disposition. Neither seek the limelight or enjoy engaging in conflict. Key differences revolve around people versus task orientation. Doves prioritize commitments to relationships as the engine of productivity; Owls focus on the accuracy and organization of tasks as the primary driver of success.

When working with Owls, Doves should keep the following in mind:

1. **Keep it formal.** Keep small talk or personal references to a minimum. Professionalism in mannerisms puts this style at ease.
2. **Do your homework.** Offer as much sequential detail and process as possible. Your high degree of subject

matter involvement is important for Owls to build trust in your competence.

3. **Set high standards.** Owls don't cut corners. Focus on what represents the highest possible quality outcome, and work backward according to resource and time restraints.

4. **Avoid feelings.** Owls are interested in your objective analysis. Any discussion around emotional concerns will suggest to this style that rational thinking has been compromised.

5. **Planning focus.** Have a detailed plan ready to share and a backup plan devised as well. This represents standard practice for Owls.

TOP TEN CONSIDERATIONS FOR DOVES

- **Comfort zones.** Challenge yourself to stretch into new areas. Remember that "failing" generally means you're getting smarter.
- **Helpful nature.** When you feel overburdened, don't just think "no," say it out loud.
- **Attachment to harmony.** Healthy, constructive candor leads to clarity for both sides, often revealing the best ideas.
- **Reticence.** Practice directing others by voicing your preferences and being persuasive.
- **Need for stability.** Developing stronger coping skills for change will be helpful to both you and others.
- **Resistance to asking for help.** When your plate is full, ask for help.
- **Long memories.** Letting go of negative memories enables greater mental agility.
- **Safety.** Experiment with different types of solutions to solve problems.
- **Focusing on people.** Become more solution focused with others.
- **Making it personal.** Switching priorities or changing your mind is normal, not an act of betrayal.

CHAPTER FIVE

Owls

———

OWL BASICS: DETAIL ORIENTED, SYSTEMATIC, ANALYTICAL, QUESTIONING

KEYWORDS THAT CAPTURE OWLS' ATTENTION:

- Perfect, meticulous, tailored, customized, organized, careful, systematic, analytical, engineered, rigor, fact-checked
- *Avoid: Random, intuition, feels right*

I once coached an Eagle chief operating officer (COO)—we'll call him Doug—who reported to an Owl CEO, Kevin. Their relationship was strained, in large part because Kevin's decision-making process featured tremendous skepticism to ideas Doug brought to the table. The CEO's reticence led to significant delays in launching initiatives, which this Eagle COO found intolerable.

After realizing his CEO's behavior was typical for high-intensity Owls, Doug tried a new strategy. At his next meeting with Kevin, Doug abandoned his typically confident I-know-this-is-right demeanor and introduced an idea *as if* he was racked with doubt. Instead of his typical high-level overview, he opened with the underlining rationale, presented multiple points of view, offered two tentative solutions, and leaned reluctantly toward Solution A as opposed to Solution B. In other words, Doug was faking it. He already knew what he wanted and how it should be executed.

After considering his COO's perspective, Kevin walked over to the whiteboard and mapped out both potential solutions. He listed the objections, issues, problems, and potential setbacks Doug had offered—all of which Kevin would have raised on his own had Doug not saved him the trouble.

Because he had deeply prepared for this meeting, Doug sat patiently and answered every question Kevin posed with ease. To his surprise, he and Kevin moved steadily through the possibilities, and the CEO came away satisfied, even enthusiastic, with the option Doug privately preferred. Doug could hardly contain his glee. After suffering through countless frustrating conversations with Kevin, Doug now knew how to win.

And win he did. Doug continued to lean toward Kevin's rigorous, logical approach—even though he was still "faking it" by pretending to be skeptical. Surprisingly, Doug witnessed their relationship improve in other areas as Kevin brought him in on wider strategic discussions.

Over the next year, however, Doug realized something almost comically ironic. Methodically analyzing potential solutions from a variety of perspectives followed by significant analysis was, in fact, leading Doug to smarter decision making. What began as exasperated fakery had gradually morphed into genuine adoption of his Owl CEO's approach. Summing up his journey with me, Doug remarked, "Clearly, the joke is on me."

Aside from being a great example of flexing to a contrasting style for superior results, this story exemplifies both what makes Owls terrific and, at times, a challenge to work with.

ACCURACY IS KING

Owl styles are on a never-ending quest for peak accuracy. Think of your Owl colleagues as the guardians of integrity. Meticulous planning, rigorous analysis, and logical reasoning represent nothing less than oxygen for this style to function well in the workplace. Environments that feature haphazard decision making, sloppy adherence to processes, and chronically shifting priorities create tremendous stress for this style.

Because Owls have the tendency to catastrophize, they're actually up at night worried about small mistakes that can cascade into big problems. So, while their precision and high expectations may be exhausting for other styles to contend with, your Owl colleague is only looking out for everyone's best interests, including yours.

SYSTEMATIC THINKING

If you want to get under an Owl's skin, start dropping the word *random* in casual conversation. Owls don't do random tasks; they create systems. It's systems that enable Owls to organize and execute efficiently. Process and procedures are the mechanisms through which Owls are able to build their way up to the big, visionary picture.

This kind of methodology is important to Owls not only in their own work but also in the work of others. While your ideas may be great, it's only through a logically thought-out process that ideas become reality. Your attention to the primary importance of logical processes is how Owls build trust, both in you and your ideas.

DEPLOYING CHANGE WITH OWLS

When confronted with change, Owls respond with questions. "Why are we doing this? Why now? What will need to be shifted, redone, or dropped? Where is the evidence this change will lead to the results we seek?" Eagle and Parrot leaders often interpret this questioning approach as an interrogation. As a result, these two styles often rationalize their *avoidance* of Owl colleagues with the following: "I've got to push this initiative forward! I don't have time to answer twenty-nine questions to justify the validity of my decision." With this mindset, leaders bring about unnecessary suffering to themselves and many others.

How does a leader transform reluctant Owls into the tip of the change spear? Bring them in early, as with Doves, and ask them to *architect* the change processes from the ground up. To put it bluntly, Owls trust themselves more than they trust you. By engaging them early and utilizing their core strengths, you will ease their concerns around the change initiative you seek.

WHAT OWLS CAN TEACH US

If you ever find yourself in the midst of a major decision, gather some Owls and ask them to lay out their worst-case scenarios. Allow them to catastrophize a bit. It may sound dramatic, but as rationally driven people, an Owl's deep concerns are born from real, logical possibilities as opposed to emotionally driven shadows in the night.

In this way, Owls will always be on the lookout for everyone's best interests and for danger along the road ahead. It may sound counterintuitive, but it's important to recognize your Owl colleague's skepticism for what it is—a strength. Just as you appreciate cautiousness from your lawyer and accountant as protecting you from exposure to unforeseen threats, come to see your Owl colleague's doubtful, unconvinced response to your wonderful ideas in the same light.

Another useful application of your Owl colleague's logical nature is as a natural-born diplomat. Because Owls don't consider emotion as evidence, they can effectively mediate disputes by dispassionately guiding both sides to a logical resolution. They're able to cut through the drama and just see the facts.

EMBRACING COMPLEXITY: THE HIDDEN GENIUS OF OWLS

This style has an innate ability to embrace and solve complex problems that require critical-thinking skills. In fact, the more intricate the issue, the more energized and engrossed an Owl style becomes. They naturally bring a rigorous, methodical approach that examines every aspect.

WHAT WE CAN TEACH OWLS

If a conversation revolves around information and data, Owls are engaging, patient listeners. However, if a conversation features emotional content, this style often misses the moment. Feelings are, essentially, a distraction from the core quality focus Owls are unearthing and evaluating when listening to someone. As a result, feelings are white noise and generally go unacknowledged. However, many Owls need to learn that listening is not about information exchange. Listening is an act of validation for the speaker, and ignoring the emotional dynamic creates a chasm the speaker will interpret as a lack of respect.

In these situations, Owls often turn people off by wearing what I call their "Spock face." This flat, unemotional, frozen facial mask inspires the assumption from other styles that Owls don't care about them when emotions run high. This isn't fair, of course. Owls *do* care, through the prism of analysis. However, people in an emotional state aren't looking for analytics. They seek emotional connection.

If you're an Owl, don't underestimate the importance of emotional validation. I once coached a sales division president who was furious his team had badly missed their quarterly numbers. He called three sales managers into his office, one of whom was an Owl style, and let them have it. As the boss vented away, the Owl went Spock face and just stared back impassively. A week later, one of those sales managers was fired. Guess which one.

After the incident, the sales leader told me, "Dan, he just didn't *get it*. I can't have that in my organization."

"Actually," I replied, "he did understand the seriousness of the situation. He just didn't know how to *signal* that he got it."

"Well," the leader responded, "if he can't convey that with me, then how could he help our clients when they're unhappy? I have no regrets."

I'm not suggesting this leader was justified, but the story illustrates the importance of validating emotions. If you're an Owl and come across as aloof, cold, and removed, you will create added stress for yourself and others when the chips are down. As we talked about earlier, we tend to like the people who make us feel we've been heard.

OWL PERFECTIONISM

According to the American Psychological Association, people who suffer from perfectionism are more likely to struggle with depression, anxiety, and a host of other mental health problems. When working in groups large and small, I ask people to raise their hand if they think they suffer from perfectionism. Without exception, the Owl groups, whether twenty or two hundred in number, dominate the raised hands.

Perfectionism prevents Owls from meeting deadlines, working well with others, and getting a good night's sleep. The solution to perfectionism is pursuing excellence instead. Striving for excellence surfaces an Owl's best thinking and efforts. Perfectionism, by contrast, is enough to drive both the Owl and everyone around him crazy.

The line between excellence and perfectionism can be difficult to identify. I advise these guardians of integrity to start off every project with an exercise. Draw a line down the middle of a piece of paper. On the left side write *Perfectionism* at the top and catalog what perfect looks like for this project. Don't hold back. Make your list as long and detailed as possible. On the right side, write *Excellence* at the top and do the same.

Your excellence list must take into account the real world, the one with limited budgets, time constraints, human error, and shifting priorities. This is not an exercise in excuse making. This column should represent genuine success. Owls who organize themselves around excellence create healthy challenges and inspire their colleagues to achieve stretch goals. Owl styles who fall down the perfectionist rabbit hole isolate themselves and create stress for their coworkers. If you're an Owl, choose carefully.

WORKING WITH AN OWL

If you happen to lack strong detail-orientation skills, don't be surprised if your Owl colleagues notice. They are simply wired to care about the small stuff more than you are, so keep yourself from getting annoyed by their choice of priorities.

Owls are adept at refining existing projects through repeated questioning. Whatever your idea is, chances are your Owl cohort will pose a number of questions that expose fault lines and potential issues. So, yes, they will rain on your parade. Embrace this *predictable* dynamic as an important pathway to sharpening your own thinking.

When listening, Owls can get silently sidetracked by a single point you made three minutes ago. While you're now on paragraph twelve, they're still trying to figure out what you said in paragraph two. A good way to prevent this is to occasionally pause and check to see they are tracking with you.

To spare yourself these experiences, try presenting your ideas in written rather than verbal form. Writing it out will likely lead to a more thorough approach on your part and give the Owl the opportunity to reflect at their pace.

MICROMANAGEMENT

It's easy to accuse Owls of being micromanagers—and, in many ways, they are. There's no doubt Owls delegate with a detailed plan in mind. It's also important to understand this is a direct result of the Owl's need for systemization. They have a process, they know it works, and they want you to benefit as well.

The problem is that other types view this as snuffing out their creativity and autonomy, as well as disarming their sense of value. To an Owl, however, a systemized approach to handing off assignments is nothing more than professionalism in action. It's their way of arming coworkers with everything they need to be successful.

DELEGATING TO AN OWL

When you are delegating to an Owl, lean toward their style. Prepare a project plan, don't leave out the details, and anticipate this style will ask more questions than you would before being satisfied that they have what is needed to move forward. Note: Your Owl colleague will probably dispense with your plan, because it doesn't meet their standards. What's important is they will appreciate the time and effort you put in to create one in the first place. If that's annoying to you, well, we suggest you develop a sense of humor about it.

Another key when delegating to this style is to make deadlines as generous as possible. The Owl's preference for longer time frames allows them to ensure the highest levels of quality.

THE STRESSED-OUT OWL

The most common source of stress for Owls is when they can't solve a problem, or the quality of a product or project is substandard. Owls are not emotionally transparent, so it can be difficult to tell when they're feeling pressured. Whereas a Parrot or Eagle will be loud and demonstrative in their stress, an Owl will just give you a look that says, "You don't understand what I understand." This can come across as condescending and typically leads to problems with coworkers.

BALANCING A STRESSED-OUT OWL

It may seem ironic to this style, but adding Parrot energy to their repertoire can be an antidote for their stress. Because Owls tend to catastrophize, Parrot optimism that "this too shall pass" is not only helpful but also has the benefit of being true.

The second gift Parrots have to offer Owls is their natural skill as knowledge networkers. Parrots enjoy the benefits of wide social and professional networks. These contacts are information sources for fresh ideas and perspectives.

Parrots can remind Owls that when you're stuck, don't reach further inward; reach outward and ask for help.

Here's an example of what can happen when there isn't any Parrot or Eagle energy in a group.

I once worked with a team of PhDs in the pharmaceutical world who create cancer drugs that save lives. Of the forty-three attendees, forty-one were Owls and two were Doves. Really.

The group had been experiencing team dynamic issues, and our discussion revolved around how to improve their internal culture. I had them write down what an ideal culture would look like, get into groups, and put their thoughts on the walls. Each participant then had to walk around the room and select two concepts most important to creating a healthier culture. The number one vote-getter by a wide margin was this: "The ability to ask questions without feeling stupid."

This department had so much internal Owl energy that they feared reaching out even to their own teammates to solve problems. That's not an issue a group of Eagles or Parrots would even recognize, but for a style that takes such personal pride in figuring things out through analysis, admitting the need for help created fear of being harshly judged by fellow Owls. The lesson is this: too much of any one style creates blind spots. Adding all perspectives to the mix is a healthy approach to improving team effectiveness.

CONFLICT

When an Owl has the facts, they will engage in conflict with a low-key persistence. However, if this style does not have enough data to reach a bulletproof conclusion, they simply won't engage. Meanwhile, other styles involve themselves much earlier in the lead-up to decisions with strong opinions that shape the outcome.

Other styles, particularly Eagles and Parrots, find it difficult to resolve conflict with Owls, because they haven't armed themselves with enough data to compete with the Owl's point of view. In addition, many issues have an emotional component Owls simply ignore. This creates added frustration, because their stoic nature can come across as condescending. The solution: when entering a contentious conversation with an Owl, come prepared, set aside as much emotion as possible, don't expect a single conversation to resolve the issue, and be persistent.

QUICK TIPS FOR INFLUENCING AN OWL

- Give Owls plenty of physical space.
- Avoid too much eye contact. Intense eye contact is a form of aggression for this style.
- Calm your voice.
- Don't overdo it on the confidence (Eagles) or the happiness (Parrots).
- Be thoughtful in your speech.
- Give Owls extra time to fully consider decisions.
- When talking, de-emphasize feelings and stick to logic.
- Avoid saying, "I feel..." Instead, try, "I *think*..."
- Articulate the process you went through to arrive at your conclusion.

THE OWL MANAGER

Whenever I encounter an Owl who manages a team of people, I ask them why they assumed that position. Almost without fail, the answer is the same. "Because it was the next step in my career." The answer is not, "Because I want to be a force for good in the careers of others." In fact, many Owls I've encountered will freely admit managing others is the biggest stressor in their professional lives and one they would prefer to do without.

Why? Because people are complicated, messy, and filled with drama. This is not the Owl's ideal sandbox to play in. Does this mean Owls shouldn't be managing other people? Not at all. It does mean, however, Owls should be prepared to stretch their capabilities significantly in a people-centric direction if they are to be effective in a manager role.

LEADERSHIP PRIORITIES

- **Rigor:** Bases decision making on data and analysis
- **Knowledge:** Skilled at explaining complex issues
- **Systematic thinking:** Strong commitment to building processes and procedures
- **Logical decision making:** Utilizes data to arrive at conclusions

LEADERSHIP CHALLENGES

- **Low energy:** May lack needed enthusiasm to capture and inspire others
- **Lack of connection:** May fail to build a guiding coalition for major decisions
- **Minutiae:** May fall into analysis paralysis
- **Hesitancy:** May be risk averse when boldness is required

BIRD BY BIRD
OWLS WORKING WITH EAGLES

Neither of these task-oriented styles requires an emotional connection to work well with others. Key differences revolve around attention to detail versus the big picture and introverted versus extroverted energy.

When working with Eagles, Owls should keep the following in mind:

1. **Be brief.** Focus on communicating what steps you want to take, not how you arrived at the decision. Bogging an Eagle down in the rigor of your analysis will only test their patience.
2. **Demonstrate confidence.** Eagles trust those who believe in themselves and their ideas. Pick up your pace, make consistent eye contact, speak with conviction, avoid a monotone delivery, and lean forward in your seat.
3. **Focus on the win.** What are the biggest contributions your efforts are making to the success of the group or mission? Avoid narrowcasting your contributions; put them in context of the team's success.
4. **Pivot quickly to changing circumstances.** Eagles will rapidly shift their priorities to meet the demands of both internal and external stakeholders. Demonstrate that you can roll with the punches.
5. **Address issues in real time.** Eagles appreciate problem solvers, not problem explainers. When an issue arises, move quickly to limit the damage and keep the project moving forward.

OWLS WORKING WITH PARROTS

The Owl and Parrot styles are on opposite ends of many

spectrums: systematic versus free flowing, stoic versus jubilant, even-paced versus fast-paced.

When working with Parrots, Owls should focus on the following:

1. **Smile.** Parrots respond well to warm communication and a more relaxed atmosphere.
2. **Big picture first.** Like Eagles, Parrots need to understand the larger context in order to organize the smaller elements of a project or mission.
3. **Be optimistic about challenges.** Just because a solution hasn't been found doesn't mean that it's not around the corner. Pessimism negates a Parrot's energy to explore what is possible.
4. **Don't deliver spreadsheets.** Parrots would much prefer a ten-minute conversation in which you summarize where you are than the forty-five minutes it would take to comb through information they won't remember anyway.
5. **Learn to trust their intuition.** Parrots are well practiced at intuitive decision making. While this approach is foreign to you, it works well for them.

OWLS WORKING WITH DOVES

Owls and Doves share an introverted nature and a methodical approach to their work lives. Both are sensitive to criticism and revert to passive-aggressive behavior in response. Key differences: Owls are task oriented; Doves are relationship oriented.

When working with Doves, Owls should focus on the following:

1. **Get to know them as people.** Doves are wired to sort out trusting relationships from the other kind. Take an interest in their hobbies and their family life. Show that you care about them as human beings, not just task executers.

2. **Relax your body language.** Like Parrots, Doves appreciate a smile and a more informal demeanor. This reduces potential friction and converts a competitive environment into a congenial one.

3. **Talk about relationships, not just tasks.** Doves understand that healthy relationships are the key to successful cultures. Focusing exclusively on tasks leaves this style cold.

4. **Pat them on the back.** Doves appreciate being appreciated. Compliment this style on their thoroughness and strong work ethic. They deserve it.

5. **Communicate decisions from a people perspective.** Doves are most concerned about the impact their decisions have on their coworkers and the culture. While systems are important to this style, people are more important.

TOP TEN CONSIDERATIONS FOR OWLS

- **Overpreparedness.** Planning is critical, but the *doing* of a complex task can be an effective teacher as well.
- **Intensity.** Smile a bit. Your laser-like focus can intimidate other styles.
- **Catastrophizing.** Even if it all fails, the sun will rise tomorrow.
- **Perfectionism.** Pursue *excellence* instead. You will make more deadlines and keep your sanity.
- **Analytical feedback.** Recognize effort as well, not just the achievement of high-quality standards.
- **Introspection.** Communicate and collaborate with those outside your immediate circle to achieve a wider range of approaches to problem solving.
- **Attachment to absolute integrity.** Just because you got it wrong doesn't mean you have failed.
- **Sensitivity to criticism.** Getting better requires thick skin.
- **Logical nature.** There's more to decision making than rational analysis. Cultivate an appreciation for spontaneity, intuition, and momentum.
- **Questioning nature.** Over questioning leads to paralysis.

CHAPTER SIX

Bird-Watching

—

One of the most common questions people have about this material is how to recognize the styles of others. We call that bird-watching. In truth, each chapter has already detailed many of the behaviors each style exhibits in the workplace. However, what about someone you don't know as well or at all?

As we'll talk about in the next chapter, many people tend to be a mix of these four basic types, and we can connect these styles in various ways. Eagles and Owls—the Dominant and Conscientious types—are more task oriented. Parrots and Doves—the Influential and Steady types—are more people oriented. Eagles and Parrots are both fast-paced and verbal, while Owls and Doves are even-paced and reserved.

The decision tree below can help you identify types, as

well as how they connect with secondary styles. We'll dive deeper into bird hybrids in the next chapter.

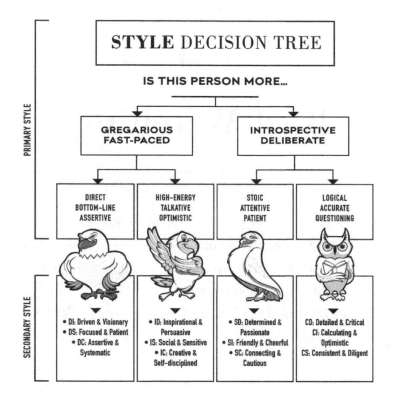

BIRD IDENTIFICATION

As you think about someone whose style you don't know through a profile, start with the obvious markers. Are they gregarious or shy, emotional or stoic, spontaneous or deliberate? What tone of voice does this person tend to use: confident or careful, lots of voice inflection or monotone? Look for cues in body language. Do they smile a lot or have a flat expression? Do they take up a lot of physical space, or do they compose themselves unobtrusively? In other words, observe and a picture will emerge naturally.

Simple practice is the best way to become a pro at determining types. I like to play a game while waiting in line at the grocery store. I observe the cashier, paying attention to the kind of energy and body language she has. Does she say hello and smile at every customer with genuine enthusiasm, or is her interaction following company protocol? Is she interacting with her coworkers in the next aisle, or is she totally focused on the task at hand? You get the idea.

Here's a list of behaviors to look for with each style:

EAGLE BIRD-WATCHING
- Speaks quickly
- Keeps statements brief
- Maintains consistent eye contact
- Has a no-nonsense demeanor
- Uses blunt, declarative statements
- Asks direct questions
- Is openly skeptical
- Advances the conversation quickly
- Leans forward when sitting
- Has confident expression
- Stands up straight

PARROT BIRD-WATCHING

- Opens with a smile
- Has upbeat, high energy
- Speaks rapidly
- Easily engages in small talk
- Shifts conversation spontaneously
- Uses a positive tone
- Focuses on people
- Is open to possibilities
- Laughs a lot
- Uses a wide range of facial expressions

DOVE BIRD-WATCHING

- Has an agreeable and welcoming manner
- Speaks with a softer tone
- Is moderate and even paced in speech and action
- Listens patiently and doesn't interrupt
- Has a calm demeanor
- Is modest when talking about himself/herself
- Develops opinions slowly
- Talks comfortably about nonbusiness subjects
- Smiles warmly
- Focuses on product/service dependability

OWL BIRD-WATCHING

- Is formal in appearance and disposition

- Maintains flat facial expression
- Speaks in monotone
- Refrains from talking about himself/herself
- Asks for detailed information
- Has already researched your product/service
- Asks questions
- Focuses on quality
- Is slower paced
- Displays caution about next steps

With practice, you'll develop your ability to pick out the bird types around you. Once you begin observing the behavior of others, you'll be able to adapt to their needs, which will improve the quality of your relationships.

OBSERVING STYLE OVERUSE

As you begin to hone your observations of style habits and markers, you may at first find it tricky to diagnose when someone is overusing their style. You may even have trouble understanding how overuse of your own style comes across to others.

The key to understanding overuse is knowing the interplay between a style's strengths and weaknesses. When we infuse our strengths with too much energy, we create corresponding weaknesses in our behaviors that are directly related. In the graphic below, we'll take a look at the overuse of each type and review key strategies for lessening its frequency and impact.

OVERUSING YOUR STRENGTHS CAUSES WEAKNESSES

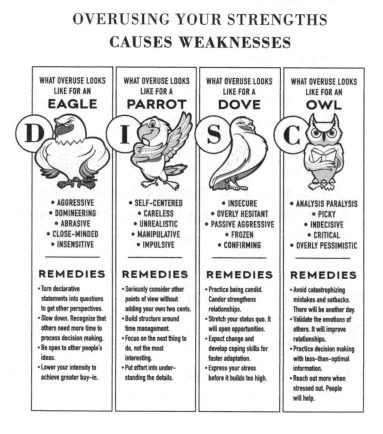

WHAT OVERUSE LOOKS LIKE FOR AN **EAGLE**	WHAT OVERUSE LOOKS LIKE FOR A **PARROT**	WHAT OVERUSE LOOKS LIKE FOR A **DOVE**	WHAT OVERUSE LOOKS LIKE FOR AN **OWL**
• AGGRESSIVE • DOMINEERING • ABRASIVE • CLOSE-MINDED • INSENSITIVE	• SELF-CENTERED • CARELESS • UNREALISTIC • MANIPULATIVE • IMPULSIVE	• INSECURE • OVERLY HESITANT • PASSIVE AGGRESSIVE • FROZEN • CONFIRMING	• ANALYSIS PARALYSIS • PICKY • INDECISIVE • CRITICAL • OVERLY PESSIMISTIC
REMEDIES	**REMEDIES**	**REMEDIES**	**REMEDIES**
• Turn declarative statements into questions to get other perspectives. • Slow down. Recognize that others need more time to process decision making. • Be open to other people's ideas. • Lower your intensity to achieve greater buy-in.	• Seriously consider other points of view without adding your own two cents. • Build structure around time management. • Focus on the next thing to do, not the most interesting. • Put effort into understanding the details.	• Practice being candid. Candor strengthens relationships. • Stretch your status quo. It will open opportunities. • Expect change and develop coping skills for faster adaptation. • Express your stress before it builds too high.	• Avoid catastrophizing mistakes and setbacks. There will be another day. • Validate the emotions of others. It will improve relationships. • Practice decision making with less-than-optimal information. • Reach out more when stressed out. People will help.

CHAPTER SEVEN

Bird Hybrids

—

Understanding each of the four bird styles in isolated depth makes their combinations easier to appreciate. Because most of us possess both a primary and secondary style, that backup influence plays a significant role in a person's behavioral makeup. For example, an Eagle-Owl has a very different lens from which to view the world than an Eagle-Parrot.

Note: A significant minority of people exhibit three types. They can be harder to read, because, by definition, they are pulling from three behavioral sources instead of two. Understanding how a person's secondary style impacts their actions can help you observe various blends of behaviors.

READING SECONDARY STYLE

Reading your coworker's secondary style can be relatively simple. Observe which bird he feeds first, then which he feeds next. Let's use an Eagle-Parrot manager as an example.

He strides into the room with focused intensity and declares, "We've got a big project coming up, and it's going to pose a challenge given our limited resources. We're looking at some tight deadlines that are going to require efficiency and accountability in order to pull this off. Let's figure out who's going to do what." Priorities, milestones, and deadlines are then established, at which point the manager visibly relaxes, smiles, and loosens his tie. "OK, that was a great meeting. Let's have a team lunch at the Lodge and relax."

First, the manager needed to ensure everyone had clarity around expectations and deliverables. With his inner Eagle satisfied, the inner Parrot was hungry for social interaction and team building.

If the manager is a Parrot-Eagle, the order simply reverses: "Today, lunch is on me," he announces. "I've booked us at the Lodge for some fun. Afterward, we're going to focus on a big project coming up." Sure enough, the afternoon is spent focusing intently on the challenging road ahead.

What follows is a brief synopsis of style blends.

EAGLE-PARROT

Eagle-Parrots represent a double dose of extroversion. They are goal-oriented, high-energy individuals who naturally command the attention of others. This style combination thinks big and is aggressive in pursuing their ambitions.

EAGLE-PARROT STRENGTHS

Eagle-Parrots excel at creating a vision with persuasive, confident communication. They thrive in dynamic, fast-paced environments that prioritize growing something new as opposed to refining what already exists. This is an individual with a high tolerance for risk-taking, because obstacles and challenges energize innate problem-solving skills. They seek as much autonomy in decision making as possible and place a strong emphasis on teamwork.

EAGLE-PARROT CHALLENGES

Eagle-Parrot intensity doesn't naturally lend itself to patience. Other styles grow weary of this combo's enthusiasm for shifting priorities on the fly. Eagle-Parrots must also remind themselves to attentively listen for more than just confirmation of their own preexisting opinions or biases. Eagle/Parrots have little patience for skepticism and can thus come across as dismissive and overly confident.

Eagle/Parrots are so focused on their goals that they often neglect the investigation required to understand the wide-ranging needs of those who actually execute their vision. Self-aware Eagle/Parrots surround themselves with Owls and Doves who are adept at creating systems and processes that ensure quality.

EAGLE-PARROTS AS LEADERS

Eagle-Parrot styles make very charismatic, high-energy leaders. They are skilled at persuasion, prioritize action over analysis, and are adept at creating a compelling vision that attracts enthusiastic followers.

They are comfortable rapidly shifting priorities to meet the demands of the day. Tapping their highly developed intuition and thirst for spontaneity, they are not afraid to take leaps of faith and shake up the status quo. They typically provide followers with significant leeway in doing their jobs and delivering results.

EAGLE-PARROT VERSUS PARROT-EAGLE

Whereas an Eagle-Parrot will emphasize results, a Parrot-Eagle will emphasize what is possible.

EAGLE-OWL

Eagle-Owls possess an internal conflict that ignites a powerful drive to succeed. The Eagle-half demands results now; the Owl-half demands the highest quality before delivering a final product. This dynamic creates an internal pressure cooker to excel at everything they do and creates high expectations that other style combinations find taxing over time.

This hybrid is part extroverted (Eagle) and part introverted (Owl), meaning that depending on the situation, your Eagle-Owl colleague can either command the spotlight or retreat quietly to the back of the room.

EAGLE-OWL STRENGTHS

Eagle-Owls are ambitious, serious, and industrious. The Eagle side has a gift for prioritizing tasks based on efficiency of execution and impact on the larger goal. The Owl side will either create or demand logical systems that ensure quality.

EAGLE-OWL CHALLENGES

An Eagle-Owl is not likely to be the most popular person in your organization. These are not "warm" and "fuzzy" colleagues or managers. Their relentless focus on task execution and quality often blinds them to competing priorities from other parts of the organization, and their intensity intimidates other styles who are more people oriented in their approach to work.

One surprising repercussion of Eagle-Owl cultures is a lack of accountability in communicating difficult issues. A culture of transactional relationships where colleagues are judged only by their ability to produce results can create a climate of fear, meaning that when things go wrong, direct reports hide the facts from Eagle-Owl managers to avoid conflict and consequences.

EAGLE-OWLS AS LEADERS

Through a combination of Eagle ambition and Owl tenacity, this combination tends to charge their way up the corporate ladder. They are a power pack of productivity.

Although not naturally adept at soft skills, Eagle-Owls can often be effective managers through their application of significant structure, clarity, and direction.

EAGLE-OWL VERSUS OWL-EAGLE

Eagle-Owls are focused on results and achieving objectives. They are relentless in their pursuit of goals. The Owl-Eagle, by contrast, is a bit more conflicted. They want to get things right the first time, which can lead to even more intensity in the service of accuracy.

PARROT-DOVE

Like their Eagle-Owl counterparts, this style blend can be confusing for others to figure out. The Parrot within loves the spotlight while the inner Dove needs alone time to recharge. The Parrot side loves to speak extemporaneously, while the Dove side is mindful that words have consequences and should be chosen carefully. It's wonderfully inconsistent.

PARROT-DOVE STRENGTHS

What's *not* confusing about this combo is both style energies love people, which makes for a likable hybrid. Warm, friendly, interested, well meaning, and curious, the Parrot-Dove is enjoyable to be around. They are sensitive to the emotional needs of others and aim to please either through being highly entertaining or patiently empathic.

PARROT-DOVE WEAKNESSES

Parrot-Doves struggle with candid conversations for fear of hurting the other person's feelings or damaging a relationship. Filling their ears with sand in hopes that everything will magically work out typically leads to bigger issues to resolve down the road. Establishing boundaries and holding others accountable when they are crossed is a source of great discomfort for this style blend. In turn, it can be difficult for others to have difficult conversations with Parrot-Doves, because they're just so nice.

PARROT-DOVES AS LEADERS

Parrot-Doves make highly effective leaders, because they intuitively know how to build trust and create an environment that gives others the room to be themselves. Parrot-Dove cultures are collegial, team oriented, optimistic, and sensitive to the morale that transforms the office into a family.

At a glance, one might guess instilling accountability in employees might present an issue for this style combination, but Parrot-Dove cultures are typically quite effective in this area. When direct reports make mistakes, they feel safe enough to openly share the situation with their Parrot-Dove managers.

PARROT-DOVES VERSUS DOVE-PARROTS

Whereas the Parrot-Dove emphasizes adventure and spontaneity, the Dove-Parrot will prioritize connection and stability over new ideas that take the group in a different direction.

DOVE-OWL

The Dove-Owl is a perfectionist hybrid. The Owl side demands rigor while the Dove side seeks to ensure that no one is negatively impacted by their work. Dove-Owls are extremely committed to methodically completing tasks and keeping their commitments at the highest level of quality. Because this hybrid represents a double dose of introversion, Dove-Owls tend to have a rich inner life, rather than being outspoken and demonstrative. This is a style blend that thinks it over, ponders a bit more, considers possible outcomes of saying something this way or that way, and only then...speaks.

DOVE-OWL STRENGTHS

When a Dove-Owl says they're going to do something, consider it done. This combination doesn't take commitments lightly. They place great emphasis on being able to deliver high-quality work that satisfies their own high standards.

DOVE-OWL CHALLENGES

This combination rarely speaks up either early or often. Humble to a fault and sensitive to rocking the boat with a dissenting opinion, this reticent approach to communication often gives the impression they are in agreement with a decision when in fact they're not. Conflict averse to a high degree, they are unlikely to speak up until a situation reaches critical mass. Unfortunately, by this point, the train has already left the station.

DOVE-OWLS AS LEADERS

With a dual focus on quality and harmony, Dove-Owl leaders are masters at creating environments that make goals achievable. They believe quality doesn't happen by accident but through careful planning and logical systems. The Dove side values a collaborative environment in which everyone has a voice and can help shape the agenda; the Owl side prizes rational analysis to secure the best results.

This blend of styles has a calm, reassuring presence that exudes quiet confidence. There is no decision that can't wait for proper vetting before being acted on, and risks are evaluated through a cautious and skeptical lens. This creates a culture that prioritizes consistency and preserving what unites the group.

DOVE-OWL VERSUS OWL-DOVE

Dove-Owls emphasize people first and the system second; Owl-Doves emphasize the analytical first and people second.

CHAPTER EIGHT

Learning from One Another

—

Humility is the pathway. Actively seeking out how people approach situations very differently than you do expands your toolbox, giving you a wider range of possible solutions to complex problems. When Eagles pay attention to Dove behaviors, they learn how to better connect with others. That's valuable. When Doves lean in an Eagle direction, they more readily stand up for what they believe, as opposed to what makes others comfortable. When Parrots work with Owls, they reap the benefits that proper planning and analysis bestows on accomplishing tasks. When Owls add Parrot perspectives to their repertoire, they're able to trust their intuition despite not having every fact at their disposal before making a decision.

As we've discussed throughout the course of this book,

each style brings tremendous strengths to the workplace. Even the people you don't like have much to teach. In fact, they may ultimately provide the most value, because how you respond to their presence is completely up to you to decide. That's what taking personal accountability for your own state of mind represents, and it's an empowered way to live your life.

Some of the most rewarding work we do is helping clients see the hidden genius within the behaviors of colleagues who otherwise drive them crazy. Let's take a final look at the hidden genius of each type.

THE EAGLE: CONFLICT ISN'T PERSONAL

Eagles are here to remind us that nine times out of ten, conflict isn't personal. This lesson is particularly important for the more sensitive among us. The Eagle's hidden genius enables them to dive in, achieve clarity, and most importantly, *move on*. So the next time you're grappling with an issue where the intensity level rises, see the moment for what is probably is—a passionate debate over *tasks* among people who care about getting things done right.

THE PARROT: OPTIMISM IS THE KEY TO OUTLOOK

Some people might scoff at optimism, but as science now proves, there is biological wisdom in happiness—and optimism is a key component to a happier outlook on life. Your brain on happiness functions at a higher level than on unhappiness. This does not mean happiness looks or sounds the same for all styles (Owl happiness doesn't resemble Parrot happiness in outward appearance), but Parrots teach us *prioritizing* happiness is not silly or frivolous. It's an important component of a healthy professional life.

DOVES: BEING RIGHT ISN'T THE POINT

Have you ever found yourself in a business meeting (or any scenario, for that matter) where you're fighting against something or someone for the sole purpose of being right? Or maybe someone is arguing against your more logical point, simply because they can't be wrong? How unnecessary is this?

Whereas Parrots know they're right when it feels right, Eagles are born right, Owls know they're right when they have the facts on their side, and Doves simply don't feel compelled to be right. This style believes in the wisdom of teams. This talent enables Doves to surface the collective intelligence of the group. Thus, the Dove's natural inclination toward humility is their key to great leadership.

OWLS: ENERGIZED BY PROBLEM SOLVING

Owls have the unique ability to dig into complex systems and figure out how to improve them. Eagles don't have the patience for this type of meticulousness. Parrots are intimidated by the expertise required to pull it off, and Doves are wary that such complexity will lead to unforeseen negative human consequences. By contrast, Owl styles bring their formidable analytical, systemization, and logical reasoning skills to bear on complex problems.

Conclusion

Steve is a sales rep for an insurance company. He is diligent, thoughtful, and persistent. Married with two young children, Steve is committed to building his business and supporting his family. His days are filled traveling to target companies that do not provide catastrophic care options for employees. Steve strongly believes the health-care products he offers are crucial for protecting families from crises such as car accidents or a cancer diagnosis. Not only do families win, but employers who offer these protections send a positive, caring message that increases employee loyalty.

It's Wednesday morning, and Steve gets up at his usual 5:00 a.m. After breakfast, he maps out his cold calls, prospect visits, and follow-ups. He reflects on the day's possibilities and notices with a slight rush of anxiety his weekly manager call with Conrad is this afternoon. To distract himself, Steve pores over his call list again and heads out for a morning run. At 12:30 p.m., Steve's attention returns to the Conrad call, and the familiar wave of unease surges. Conrad is a fifteen-year veteran of the company and worked his way to management from the ground up. In fact, Conrad had Steve's sales territory when he started out in the business. When applying for the job, Steve thought this was a positive. Certainly, Conrad would know how to help Steve succeed in his old territory.

Unfortunately, connecting with his sales manager had been problematic from day one. Conrad had a commanding presence, and his communication style ranged from forceful to blunt. While Steve carefully considered ambiguities and possibilities before arriving at a decision, Conrad immediately seized on a particular path and hammered his perspective with conviction, all within seconds. This frustrated Steve, who preferred to methodically understand the logic behind a decision before taking action. Furthering their lack of connection, Conrad always got straight down to business, never once opening up about his personal life or taking much interest in Steve's. Months into the job, he still isn't sure if Conrad is married or single. For Steve, a call with Conrad feels like jumping on a fast-moving train furiously racing into a tunnel.

Greatly adding to his stress with Conrad is Steve's own performance—he isn't closing accounts. While adept at cultivating new contacts and building relationships, Steve has noticed a disturbing pattern that inevitably leads to stalled prospects rather than paying clients. This is devastating, because with the exception of a small travel stipend, Steve's compensation is 100 percent commission based. After two months without pay, his stress level is reaching a breaking point. On this chilly Wednesday morning, a number of troubling thoughts are running through his head. *How am I going to pay the rent? Should I quit? Get a real job with a salary? Why is Conrad so dismissive and uninterested? He clearly doesn't care about me. He never asks about my family. Our seven-minute calls don't help me at all.*

Little does Steve know, within the course of the next thirty minutes, he will have a conversation that could very well change his life. Why? Because Steve may quit, or he may persevere and eventually flourish. The truth is, Conrad is fully capable of helping Steve correct his mistakes and break out of his funk, but that critical connection is hidden in their stunted relationship.

Unfortunately, what is likely to happen is simply more of what has already transpired. Steve will report his lack of progress, and Conrad will dispense "advice" with the alacrity of a drill sergeant barking orders. Steve will think this guy is the worst manager he has ever had: a blank, impenetrable wall. In fact, this whole job feels like a wall. The cold calls, drop-ins, and contrived, agenda-driven conversations with strangers masquerading as "relationship building." It's *all* a giant wall. With his family depending on him, Steve will fight his feelings of helplessness and resume his daily grind. Or, he'll simply quit.

As we know by now, the only wall is in Steve's mind.

In reality, there are nothing but doors in his life, from Conrad to his prospects. All Steve needs are the keys. The *right* keys. Steve desperately needs the relationships in his professional world to help him grow a career and prosper financially so that he and his family can enjoy the fruits of a meaningful life. Just like you and me. But in order to achieve this, Steve has to identify the real issue, because while he thinks his problem is closing sales, it's actually much deeper than that. Steve doesn't understand how to *connect* with his boss or his potential prospects.

Let's give this story the happy ending that actually occurred.

Conrad and Steve learn about the birds and a few lightbulbs go off. What's remarkable about Eagles is how quickly they change once it's clear how to transform a likely loss into a big win. Conrad decides in order to hit his sales goals, he needs Steve to succeed, which requires an adjustment in his Eagle approach toward Steve's Dove-Owl style.

In preparation for their next call, which is now a face-to-face meeting, Steve is to come prepared with as many questions as he can, along with a log of all his activities over the last three months. Conrad prepares a detailed best practices manual tailored to his territory. It's a tedious exercise, but Conrad concludes he can use the same blueprint with others, so it's a wise investment for both Steve and future sales associates.

In their meeting, Steve is pleasantly surprised at how patiently Conrad answers his questions with an expert's depth. Steve, in turn, commits to significantly increase the volume of his cold calls, his attendance at networking events, and his focus on proper closing techniques. Shifting from poor performance to success is going to require bold action, mistakes, and learning, followed by more bold action.

Over the next six weeks, Steve and Conrad develop a brisk, practical approach to meetings. Steve is careful to hold back the details and keep his points clear and action oriented. Conrad invests more time coaching with an emphasis on specific situations and the rationale behind his approach. Ten weeks after their breakthrough meeting, Steve lands a major client with a number of other prospects moving in a positive direction. He and his manager go out for a drink with an in-the-trenches respect built on both sides.

Lessons: Their issues were never personal. Conrad was

not a jerk, and Steve was not lacking the capability to rise to the challenge. Once they simply understood what made the other tick, solutions easily presented themselves. Hey, Eagle, slow down a little. Hey, Dove-Owl, take a risk, fail, and get smarter. A PhD in psychoanalysis was not required, nor a meditation retreat. Small adjustments in behavior that honored each other's perspective built trust. When reciprocated, momentum increased, the relationship improved, and positive hidden potential revealed itself.

In the end, the quality of our lives boils down to our connection with others. There will be those we click with naturally and others who will take more effort—a lot more effort—in order to get along. It's likely this latter set offers the most personal growth, precisely because of the challenges they pose to our way of thinking and being. It's these relationships that expand our worldview and provide us with new vantage points and coping skills.

Yes, expanding our behaviors to better match those who are very different from us is daunting, but the payoff is tremendous. We turn latent energy into kinetic energy. We release hidden potential in a wide range of relationships that deliver surprising value to our lives. We gain perspective on ourselves and insights on how to bring out the best in others. We capture the true competitive advantage, and the result may very well be a more meaningful life.

About the Author

 **DAN SILVERT** is the president of Velocity Advisory Group, an executive coach, keynote speaker, and strategic advisor. He is the coauthor of *Taking Flight!*, published in nine languages, and has worked with a wide range of organizations including Aflac Insurance, Genentech, Homeland Security, Johnson & Johnson, and Zara.